Flame IN THE Mind

Flame in the Mind

A JOURNEY OF SPIRITUAL PASSION

Michael Marshall

Foreword by the Archbishop of Canterbury

ZONDERVAN™

GRAND RAPIDS, MICHIGAN 49530 USA

ZONDERVAN™

A Flame in the Mind
Copyright © 2002 by Michael Marshall

Requests for information should be addressed to:

Zondervan, *Grand Rapids, Michigan 49530*

Marshall, Michael, 1936-
    Flame in the mind : a journey of spiritual passion / Michael Marshall; foreword by the Archbishop of Canterbury.
        p. cm.
    Includes bibliographical references.
    ISBN 0-00-713095-3
    1. Len—Meditations. 2. Christian life—Meditations. 3. Augustine, Saint, Bishop of Hippo—Meditations. 4. Anglican Communion—Prayer-books and devotions—English. I. Title.
BV85 .M34 2003
242'.34—dc21

                                                                    2002009709

All Scripture quotations, unless otherwise indicated, are taken from the *New Revised Standard Version Bible,* copyright © 1989 by the Division of Christian Education of the National Council of the Churches of Christ in the USA, and are used with permission. All rights reserved.

The poem 'Out of the Chaos of My Doubt' by Mervyn Peake is used by permission. Copyright © 1972 by Faber and Faber.

The words of the hymn on page 14 by Michael Hewlett (1916–) from 'English Praise 1975' by permission of Oxford University Press.

The poem 'East Coker' by T.S. Eliot is used by permission. Copyright © 1940 by Faber and Faber.

Excerpt from 'East Coker' in *Four Quartets,* copyright 1940 by T.S. Eliot and renewed 1968 by Esme Valerie Eliot, reprinted by permission of Harcourt, Inc.

Excerpt from *Zeal of Thine House* by Dorothy L. Sayers is used by permission. Copyright © 1938 by Victor Gollancz.

Interior design by Todd Sprague

Printed in the United Kingdom

02 03 04 05 06 07 08 /❖ CLY/ 10 9 8 7 6 5 4 3 2 1

*To wonderful friends and fellow travellers
on the road of faith.*

What is a man, but his friends and his loves?
—*Augustine*

Contents

Acknowledgements

Undertaking to write a 'travel' book, albeit a 'spiritual' one, before having arrived at the principle destination, could well be construed as ambitious at best or positively pretentious at worst. However, I have been careful throughout to make frequent reference to esteemed fellow travellers who from experience know far more about the 'journey' than I do. Principle among my fellow pilgrims is of course St Augustine. I wish to make it clear from the outset that I am no scholar of Augustine, yet deeply indebted as all Augustinian enthusiasts are to the immensely scholarly and readable work of Peter Brown whose life of St Augustine was first given to me as a birthday present in 1972, a few years after its publication. My indebtedness to Peter Brown is evident on nearly every page of the book.

For the past thirty years I have collected as many of Augustine's works as I could lay my hands on together with many books about Augustine in what, on any reckoning, must now be considered a very considerable Augustine library. In the bibliography I have suggested a mere handful of books for any readers of this book to refer to if my book is at all successful in teasing others to become Augustinian enthusiasts.

The writing of any book is necessarily a team effort from start to finish. I wish to acknowledge with gratitude my deep indebtedness to Jane Collins who graciously undertook a radical re-ordering of the first very rough and ready manuscript and who practically wrote in their entirety the helpful questions for reflections and discussion at the end of each chapter. I also wish to thank Amy Boucher Pye for her editorial patience as well as Angela Scheff who handled all the nitty-gritty of references and editorial detail with such painstaking care. It was in the final stages of chasing little points of detail and abstruse references that Canon Peter Strange proved to be so immensely helpful – at the end of a telephone and always coming up with the 'answers' in record time.

Foreword by the Archbishop of Canterbury

In this, the last Lent book I shall have commissioned as Archbishop of Canterbury, I am delighted that Augustine of Hippo – arguably the most influential of all the Doctors of the Church – is the subject of Bishop Michael Marshall's perceptive and accessible book. And Bishop Michael has brought to his task all the skills and talents that have made him such an effective communicator down the years.

Now, let's be honest. None of us finds the Christian life easy. But neither did Augustine. Indeed, very little in his early life would have led anyone to contemplate for a second the idea that this brilliant man would become one of the greatest and holiest of Christian teachers. Using Augustine's turbulent journey as a model, Bishop Michael rightly encourages us to view the spiritual life as an ongoing and dynamic journey in which openness to change and growth is essential. It was, the author suggests, a life-long process of 'dislocation' and 'relocation', moving him ultimately through and beyond things temporal to things eternal.

With Augustine's pilgrimage in mind, Bishop Michael invites us to reflect intentionally and prayerfully on our own life stories. Where are you on your spiritual journey? What have been the major turning points or surprises on the way? What do you understand your ultimate destination to be? How have you experienced the Holy Spirit on your journey? These are just a few of the important questions that are posed through the course of this well-written and insightful book – questions that can take us to a deeper level of contemplation about our faith.

Whether reading this book on your own or with a group, I think you will be both challenged and inspired. The book is organized so that you can read one chapter for each week of Lent (not including the prologue and epilogue). I would encourage you to do just that. Spend some time prayerfully considering and, if reading it with a group, discussing the material in this book. As Bishop Michael suggests, draw a spiritual timeline, contemplating where you've been, where you are and where you're heading, looking for God's hand at work in your life and praying with Augustine: '. . . grant that I may not stop seeking you when I am weary, but seek your presence ever more fervently.'

+George Carey

Archbishop of Canterbury

Prologue

FLAME IN THE MIND

O Thou who camest from above,
The pure celestial fire to impart,
Kindle a flame of sacred love
On the mean altar of my heart.

Those words written by Charles Wesley in the eighteenth century capture the central image of this book and could well have been written by St Augustine of Hippo, our principal travelling companion on the spiritual journey we will take together in the course of the following chapters.

St Augustine of Hippo (AD 354–430) – to be distinguished from that other Augustine of Canterbury, who lived some two hundred years later – was consistently, throughout his life, the disciple of passion. Although he had a brilliant intellect, the driving force throughout his many years of discipleship was unquestionably a 'restless heart', on fire with love for God and for others. St Augustine's crest is always depicted as a heart with the flames of love coming out of it, sometimes with a copy of the Scriptures superimposed on that image. Passionate in both his life and his preaching, he saw the need to undertake the longest journey in the world – the journey of faith. For some people that journey originates in the mind, but for everybody it must also pass via the heart, until ultimately our wills are fired for a life of witness and service.

The phrase 'flame in the mind' was first used in the early second century AD by one of the great teachers and apologists of the Early Church, Justin Martyr (c.100–c.165). Justin was one of the most effective early communicators of the Christian faith and saw the need to bring together faith and reason. A faith rooted in heart and mind, he believed, would fire the will, transforming self-centred lives into lives lived for others as well as in the service of God. All this is the work of the Holy Spirit. From those tongues of fire at the first Pentecost in Jerusalem some two thousand years ago, the Holy Spirit has continued to warm the hearts of Christian disciples and to fire their wills with the flame of love. The very first manifestation by which God revealed himself to Moses in the Old Testament was the burning bush, which burned but was not consumed by its own fire. It is not surprising, therefore, that the image of the fire of the Holy Spirit has been central to every Christian tradition and in all the churches down the centuries. A twentieth-century hymn-writer captures the traditional image in a Pentecost hymn:

> Pray we then, O Lord the Spirit,
> On our lives descend in might;
> Let thy flame break out within us,
> Fire our hearts and clear our sight,
> Till white-hot in thy possession,
> We, too, set the world alight.[1]

WORTH HIS WEIGHT IN GOLD

St Augustine certainly 'set the world alight', not only in his own lifetime, but for centuries to come, through his passionate, enlightened teaching and preaching in the insignificant township of Hippo.[2] Indeed, he used to say that good preaching was a matter of 'one heart on fire, setting another heart on fire'.

Considering the comparative difficulties of communication in the declining years of the Roman Empire, it is simply amazing that Augustine's reputation as a scholar, teacher, writer and preacher was known in his lifetime throughout the greater part of the world of Late Antiquity. He was a legendary figure. History tells us that after Augustine died in AD 430, a group of African bishops took his body with them when they were fleeing from the Vandals. The body was subsequently deposited in Sardinia, where it remained until the eighth century. Then, on payment of gold equalling the weight of Augustine's body, a king of Lombardy brought it to Pavia, where it was buried. (Augustine was literally 'worth his weight in gold', which is where the saying comes from.) His body still lies in the church of Ciel D'oro in Pavia, where countless pilgrims visit the shrine.

Humanly speaking, Augustine should have been dead and buried and largely forgotten long ago. Much of his writing is frankly tedious and bears the limitations implicit in the prevailing culture of his day. Nonetheless, through his teaching and writing he lives on and has influenced all the various traditions within the Christian Church, East and West alike, from his own day until now. Every so often, as you read Augustine, the words spring off the page with eloquence and vitality – totally relevant to the lives of contemporary disciples hundreds of years later. All theologians, whether of the Catholic or Reformed tradition, have cause to return to Augustine. Indeed, it is possible to trace a theological and spiritual trail from St Paul through to Martin Luther via the writings and influence of Augustine – a trail which stretches on from Luther to the present day.

A MAN FOR OUR TIME?

It must be admitted, however, that much of his writing is not especially reader-friendly for the non-professional theologian. His style is heavy and quite often obscure. Trained as a rhetorician, his writings (even his letters) still bear the marks of the somewhat pompous and self-conscious style of speech delivered at the Imperial Court, where Augustine was professor for a little while in the years before his baptism. Clearly his outlook and priorities are limited by – though never totally confined to – the world of his day and to the culture in which he lived and worked. At times, for example, we feel that we have encountered a man who is afraid of his sexual urges and negative about women. Such passages, however, have to be read in the context of the hot-blooded and passionate personality of Augustine. It was precisely because he was so very hot-blooded that he had to discipline his emotions and passions. He would be astonished by the contradictory messages coming out of our Western world today, where advertisements, magazines and entertainment blatantly stimulate the passions (especially the sexual drive within all of us) while at the same time giving the impression that we should remain cool and detached in the face of all that highly erotic stimulus. Perhaps Augustine and the contemporary approach are both wrong, yet it is refreshing to see that our own culture does not have all the answers and can still learn so much from a man from an earlier age and a very different cultural setting.

Certainly, the real person of Augustine as a man for all seasons still comes through in his writings – notably in his spiritual autobiography, the *Confessions*. In that book he refuses to accept the stereotyping of authentic Christian discipleship and is at pains to show his weaknesses along with his strengths. It is for that reason that he can act as a kind of guide for pilgrims and disciples even in our own day. His profound insights into his own complex and contradictory make-up also smack of a post-Freudian psychology. For these and many other reasons we will do well to draw alongside Augustine as we set out on the spiritual journey outlined in this book.

There are other ways, too, in which Augustine speaks especially meaningfully to our own age. During his lifetime the Roman Empire was falling apart at the seams. As a result of this, Augustine lived at a time of notable resurgence in all kinds of religious cults and superstitions – a resurgence not unlike the one occurring today. We would be wise to remember the words of Rabbi Jonathan Sachs, who said, 'Religion is not always a good thing. Usually it speaks to the best in us, but it can sometimes speak to the worst. Religion is like fire. It warms, but it also burns; and we are the guardians of the flame.'[3]

Augustine fell prey to many of these cults in the course of his own searching, and then, as so often happens, after he was baptized and received into the Church, he became at times violently passionate about rooting out and even persecuting other Christians whom he felt were not sufficiently orthodox. Heresy nearly always breeds a reaction expressed in oppressive fundamentalism. Rose Macaulay, herself a convert to Christianity in mid-life, speaks of this intolerance in one of her novels:

> The Church grew so far, almost at once, from anything which can have been intended, and became so blood-stained and persecuting and cruel and warlike, and made small and trivial things so important, and tried to exclude everything not done in a certain way and by certain people, and stamped out heresies with such cruelty and rage. And this failure of the Christian church, of every branch of it in every country, is one of the saddest things that has happened in all the world. But it is what happens

when a magnificent idea has to be worked out by human beings who do not understand much of it but interpret it in their own way and think they are guided by God, whom they have not yet grasped.[4]

THE LONGEST JOURNEY IN THE WORLD

And so to our own journey. Throughout this book we shall be travelling with St Augustine on that long journey from head to heart and from heart to will. An overview of the whole journey is summed up in the well-known prayer of Augustine:

O God, you are the light of the minds that know you,
The joy of the hearts that love you,
And the strength of the wills that serve you.
Grant us so to know you that we may truly love you;
And so to love you that we may fully and freely
    serve you,
Whose service is perfect freedom,
In and through Jesus Christ our Lord. Amen.

It is a long journey indeed, in which conversion is not a one-off event but rather a continuous process. Augustine undoubtedly experienced a telling and life-changing conversion moment in the garden (see page 31), but the struggle did not end at that point. Charting the course of Christian discipleship is an unpredictable business and the Holy Spirit, like the wind, 'blows where it chooses' (John 3:8). In many ways, one of Augustine's motives in writing his *Confessions* was precisely to deny that what had happened in the garden that day signalled the end of all his problems. Far from it: Augustine still had to struggle with sins, weakness and failings after his baptism. The great Augustine scholar Peter Brown writes, 'The amazing Book Ten of the *Confessions* is not the affirmation of a cured man; it is the self-portrait of a convalescent.' He also comments, 'In Book VIII . . . the problem of the will leaps into focus. For here [after Augustine has recorded his dramatic experience in the garden], with all his difficulties resolved, with a "definite feeling of sweetness" claiming his loyalty to the Catholic faith, we meet Augustine still trapped in the habits of a lifetime; it is as if we had thought we had reached a plateau, only to find this last peak towering before us.'[5]

The stories of other people's personal journeys of faith do at least provide us with a rough and ready kind of itinerary, with some useful map readings and compass bearings as we set out on our own exploration. Every disciple would do well to have the occasional biography of a former disciple as bedside or 'roadside' reading. Yet at best the record of such other journeys of faith can perhaps only help us to recognize some signposts as we travel – and, in all honesty, those signposts and references tend to make more sense retrospectively, as we look back on our journey of discipleship, rather than prospectively, as we are preparing to set out. The true disciple who is seeking a mature faith in God will frequently be bewildered, confused and even disappointed on coming to a fork in the road or, worse, to a dead end. At such times there is always the temptation to revert to formalism, to play it strictly by the book, or even to attempt to replicate the faith journeys of other disciples as recorded in their biographies or as presented (neatly packaged) from the pulpits of well-known evangelists.

So it is not true to say that we shall be following in Augustine's footsteps, not least because that would be the very opposite of what he would have wanted. Discipleship is a very personal matter. That, of course, is not the same as saying that it is a private matter. As we travel, the Epistle to the Hebrews reminds us, we are surrounded by a 'great ... cloud of witnesses' from all ages (Hebrews 12:1). We are not travelling alone. That is a comforting thought, especially when the going gets tough or when we have lost our way. At such times it is helpful to know that other heroes of the Christian faith have trodden a similar road and have been through similar trials, yet have finally arrived at their destination, victorious through all their struggles. Augustine will therefore be our companion and, at times, our guide. He can also help to keep us on the move. As he said in his 'Sermon on Psalm 40:5': 'The man journeying to his own country must not mistake the inn for his home.'

There are six chapters to the book, on the assumption that participants in a Lent course will study one chapter a week – and this can apply whether you are working through it as an individual or as part of a group. It would surely be helpful to read the 'Introduction to Augustine' (pages 21–36) at the outset, as it gives a brief outline of Augustine's life and struggles. Each chapter ends with a prayer of Augustine, a set of questions for personal reflection, some suggested points for group discussion, and a Bible passage to meditate upon.

In one of his late sermons, St Augustine reflects eloquently on how a disciple or pilgrim might discover a proper confidence for safe travel: 'Walk in the footsteps of this man (Christ) and you will come to God. Look for no other way to come to God except this one. For if he had not himself become a way, we should always go astray. So I do not say to you, look for the way. This way comes to you itself; rise up and go!'[6]

An Introduction
to Augustine

THE CONFESSIONS

The town of Souk Ahras in eastern Algeria, some sixty miles inland from the Mediterranean, marks the site of the ancient town of Thagaste where Augustine was born on 13 November AD 354. His life story is immortalized for us in one of the greatest masterpieces of Western literature. Augustine began writing the *Confessions* in his mid-forties, shortly after he had been consecrated as Bishop of Hippo in AD 395. It relates the story of Augustine's spiritual journey, from his earliest memories through to his baptism, his ordination to the priesthood and then to the episcopate. It is most certainly not the story of a 'flash' conversion or the record of instant Christian discipleship and sanctification. Rather, it is the story of a long and painful struggle from Augustine's earliest years to midlife, with the strong implication that the journey, at the time of going to press, is far from completed.

The dramatic turning point in the book is, of course, the celebrated moment of conversion in July AD 386, when the 32-year-old Augustine heard a voice instructing him: '*Tolle, lege*' – 'Pick up and read.' When he opened a copy of the Scriptures, lying close at hand, the words from Paul's Epistle to the Romans sprang off the page: 'Not in revelling and drunkenness, not in debauchery and licentiousness, not in quarrelling and jealousy. Instead, put on the Lord Jesus Christ' (Romans 13:13).

Undoubtedly that moment, rather like St Paul's Damascus road experience, represented a significant turning point in Augustine's life. Nonetheless, although it was obviously more dramatic and memorable than many of the other turning points in his life, it is clearly wrong to see it apart from the fuller picture of a life of struggle, restlessness and searching discipleship. What we have here is the slow, unfolding conversion of the heart. That event in the garden did not mark the end of Augustine's search, but a new beginning in the long story of his discipleship. 'When human beings have finished, they are just beginning' (Sirach 18:7). Augustine deliberately lays bare his heart in the *Confessions*, partly to counter rumours of his own sanctity and to set his famed 'conversion' within the fuller context of a lifelong – and sometimes reluctant – discipleship. In the jargon of spirituality, we might say that the *Confessions* should be seen as a study not only of a once-for-all justification, but also of a longer process of sanctification.

In our own lives, in this age of the quick fix – with everything instant, from coffee to communication – we need to revisit and spell out the bewildering implications of lifelong journeying, growth and development. Although there are some Christians who talk rather glibly and superficially about conversion as a one-off and once-for-all event which transfers us instantly from the kingdom of darkness to the kingdom of light, they still have to come to terms with the lifelong struggle of faith described so well by St Paul: 'For I do not do the good I want, but the evil I do not want is what I do' (Romans 7:19).

OUR HEART'S DESIRE

The age of St Augustine, who lived a comparatively long life, is conspicuous as an age of decline, increasingly evident in social, political and spiritual chaos. The Roman Empire was fragmenting, and Augustine reflects in his own life the restlessness of his age, not least in many aspects of his personal spiritual journey. At such confused times in history, we see religion take on its most insidious and perverted forms. As Peter Brown the great scholar of the Late Antiquity points out in his work *Religion and Society in the Age of St Augustine,* it was an age of superstition and the proliferation of religious cults, a situation which was reflected in the doctrinal conflicts of the Catholic Church, both East and West. It was an age – once again not unlike our own – when the unacceptable face of perverted religion was all too much in evidence, yoked as it frequently was then with the abuse of political power.

It was in such a climate that Augustine spent the first thirty-three years of his life searching and shopping around the supermarket of religious and philosophical options so prevalent in his day. During those years he also pursued a career as an ambitious and rather successful professor of rhetoric. The son of a remarkable mother (St Monica) and a spiritually indifferent father (Patricius), Augustine was an intellectually promising youngster from the start. At an early age he went to university – first to the very provincial university of Madaura, in Algeria, and later, at the age of seventeen, to the great seaport town of Carthage, which was still regarded at that time as the second city of the Roman Empire. Carthage (modern Tunis) was a city notorious for every kind of impropriety. Augustine tells us in his *Confessions*: 'I went to Carthage, where I found myself in the midst of a hissing cauldron of lust.'[1]

Unquestionably, life in Carthage was to prove far more exciting than the frustrating early teenage years spent at home with his mother Monica. From Augustine's birth, Monica had been intensely (some might say, compulsively) zealous for her son's conversion to the Christian faith. This driving force persisted for thirty-three years, until finally Augustine was baptized just a few weeks before his mother's unexpected and premature death.

During his time as a student at Carthage, Augustine tells us that he had 'not yet fallen in love'. Rather he 'was in love with the idea of it', not unlike so many youngsters through the ages. Despite constant 'warnings' from his mother, back home in Thagaste, 'not to commit fornication and above all not to seduce any man's wife', Augustine freely tells us, in his somewhat exaggerated and self-conscious style, how he refused to choose the 'safe path'. He preferred instead 'the muddied stream of friendship, with the filth of lewdness, clouding its clear waters with hell's black river of lust.' He was intent on kicking over the traces and (to use his own words) on 'cutting a fine figure in the world'.[2]

Augustine relates how, throughout those years, he followed the dictates of his heart and his undirected desires. 'I began to look around for some object for my love, since I badly wanted to love something. I had no liking for the safe path without pitfalls, for although my real need was for You, my God, who are the food of my soul, I was not aware of this hunger.' Instead, 'to love and to have my love returned', he confessed later in life, 'was my heart's desire, and it would be all the sweeter if I could also enjoy the body of the one whom I loved.'[3]

Throughout the rest of his teenage years and into his twenties, Augustine was thus intent on following the desires of his heart and mind, strongly fired by ambition and the need to impress. Although he never 'took another man's wife', as far as we know, he did take a mistress, whose name is not revealed, and he fathered an illegitimate son when he was just eighteen. Ironically, he named his son Adeodatus – God's gift.

'In those days I lived with a woman, not my lawful wedded wife but a mistress whom I had chosen for no special reason, but that my restless passions had alighted on her. But she was the only one and I was faithful to her,' he writes.[4]

Meanwhile, Augustine was beginning to realize some of his academic ambitions, first as an outstanding student and then as a teacher of rhetoric at Carthage at the tender age of thirty. He was all set to 'cut a fine figure' in the world of academia. Within only a few years he reached even greater heights when he sailed from Carthage with his mistress and his son to the port of Ostia, near Rome. He travelled on from there to Milan, where he was soon appointed to the highly esteemed post of professor of rhetoric on the very doorstep of the royal court.

HIDE AND SEEK

Despite all this hard work, however, neither human love, the love of scholarship or worldly success satisfied his inner quest. From a young age, Augustine found himself on another journey, and it was not a geographical one. It was really a series of journeys, and they were essentially spiritual explorations of the inner life, in which heart and mind were to wrestle for supremacy. Augustine pinpoints the age of nineteen as 'the age at which I had first begun to search in earnest for truth and wisdom and had promised myself that, once I had found them, I would give up all vain hopes and mad delusions which sustained my futile ambitions'.[5]

Although these spiritual journeys originated largely in Augustine's mind, they were to prove to be very long journeys indeed. As Morpheus says in the movie *The Matrix*, 'Sooner or later, Neo, you are going to realize there's a difference between knowing the path and walking the path.' Yes, indeed! Perhaps the longest journey in the world is from head to heart, and from heart to will. A living faith enlightens the mind, warms the heart and fires the will. On that inner journey there are many turning points, significant people and mentors at each turn of the road, and many influences – sometimes conflicting – which determine direction and discernment. We shall be exploring and examining some of these influences in the course of this book, while also exploring some of the choices and challenges which are common to ourselves and Augustine. Augustine's spiritual geography may act as a kind of grid in relation to our own stories: while each person's journey will be unique, shared reference points can offer helpful guidance along the way.

Whatever else Augustine was, he was essentially a deeply religious, introspective and questioning character, with raging and conflicting passions of mind and heart, and a stubborn will. Although he had never been baptized as a child, the son of St Monica could scarcely have been anything other than deeply religious in outlook. After all, she prayed for her son from the time of his conception until the day of his baptism in AD 387, at the hands of Ambrose, Bishop of Milan. Yet Augustine's quest did not lead straight to the waters of baptism. In an age of many religious cults and superstitions, Augustine's pilgrimage of faith led him to 'pick and mix' and to flirt with all kinds of competing and conflicting spiritualities, philosophies and religious practices.

Augustine's first mentor was none other than the Roman classical orator Cicero, whose writings he came across in the course of his prescribed studies during his third year as a student at Carthage. Marcus Tullius Cicero was a famous orator, philosopher and statesman in Rome at the time of Julius Caesar, when the Roman Empire was at its height. A brilliant orator, he was in many ways a kindred spirit of Augustine. Doubtless Augustine saw much in the figure of Cicero that he wished to emulate – and in any case, the young student was looking for a role model and a hero. Thus, he tells us, 'in the usual course of the syllabus, I had reached a book by Cicero: its style was admired by almost all, though its message was ignored.' The book in question was *The Hortensius,* the discovery of which by the eager young Augustine was to be a significant signpost on his spiritual journey. He tells us in impassioned tones:

> This book indeed changed all my way of feeling. It changed my prayers to thee, O Lord. It gave me entirely different plans and aspirations. Suddenly all empty hope for my career lost its appeal; and I was left with an unbelievable fire in my heart, desiring the deathless qualities of Wisdom, and I made a start to rise up and return to Thee ... I was on fire, my God, on fire to fly away from earthly things to Thee.[6]

It was clearly quite a significant turning point. Yet, of course, fully fledged and mature Christian disciples do not fly away from earthly things in their affections, but seek to redirect them heavenwards. All that, however, was still in the future for our restless and somewhat erratic hero. Augustine's encounter with the writings of Cicero clearly challenged him, however: 'It altered my outlook on life ... provided me with new hopes and aspirations. All my empty dreams suddenly lost their charm and my heart began to throb with a bewildering passion for the wisdom of eternal truth.' Notice how powerfully Augustine transfers his affections and passions. We shall see how this becomes the driving force of his quest, fired from the heart at every stage of the journey of faith which was to dominate his whole life. A 'restless heart' indeed.

It was during his time in Carthage that Augustine also encountered the Manichees, and he became a 'Hearer', or novice, for some nine years.

The Manichees were a small sect with a sinister reputation. They were illegal; later, they would be savagely persecuted. They had the aura of a secret society; in foreign cities, Manichees would lodge only with members of their own sect; their leaders would travel around a network of 'cells' scattered all over the Roman world. Pagans regarded them with horror, orthodox Christians with fear and hatred. They were the 'Bolsheviks' of the fourth century; a 'fifth column' of foreign origin bent on infiltrating the Christian church, the bearers of a uniquely radical solution to the religious problems of the age.[7]

The more you study the dualism of Manichaeism, the more you realize that such a religious philosophy will always be current in ages of fragmentation. The fourth century AD was one such age, and so is the twenty-first century with its polarization between matter and spirit. In ages of agnosticism and atheism, people do not end up believing in nothing. Rather, they prefer to believe in anything and, like drowning men, grasp at straws of seductive and dangerous half-truths frequently packaged and marketed in the name of religion. Today we are seeing the multiplication of hundreds of religious sects and cults which enjoy huge followings, frequently among younger people. Even the current pop culture takes on semi-religious characteristics and significance in the words of its lyrics, and in the environment and culture of the discos where its 'philosophy' is marketed. 'New Age' has enjoyed an amazing popularity in recent years, judging by the number of new titles to be seen in the growing 'religious' sections in many bookshops. As we shall see later, human beings are compulsive worshippers, constantly and naively in pursuit of something or somebody to follow.

Such a climate inevitably produces religious cults and movements for which restless spirits, fascinated as well as tormented by the conflict between the material world and the spiritual world, are a ready prey. A Manichaean psalm book puts this conflict in the starkest of terms, a conflict which Augustine knew only too well from his own experience:

> I have known my soul and the body that lies upon it,
> That they have been enemies since the creation of
> the world.[8]

Clearly such religious sentiments rang all kinds of bells with Augustine's passionate and confused temperament. The genius of full-blooded sacramental and scriptural Christianity is to be found in its ability to bring together and to hold in tension soul and body, spirit and matter, in a holistic and sacramental view of the universe. It was to be a very long time, however, before Augustine would discover for himself this 'more excellent way' of perceiving both himself and the whole created order through the redemptive work of Christ's incarnation, by which the Spirit was enfleshed in the person of Jesus, Son of God and child of Mary – fully divine, yet fully human.

For no less than nine years, Augustine pursued his discipleship within the fold of Manichaeism, much to the chagrin of his mother, who followed closely on Augustine's heels to Rome and Milan. Yet by the time he reached the pinnacle of his career at Milan in AD 384, Augustine was already a disillusioned young man, not least with the ready-made and neatly packaged Wisdom on offer from the Manichees. The certainties of his youthful discipleship were beginning to dissolve, as once again – this time with the benefit of hindsight – he took up his continuing quest for Truth. This could not, and would not, be handed to him on a plate.

At the same time, Augustine came to realize that no amount of speculation could in itself attain to the truth. As he was to write later,[9] it is necessary for all seekers to use some form of 'authority' to point the way on the fog-bound highways of worldly knowledge. Speculation needs to be met by revelation, that is, by God reaching out and showing the way in Jesus, who claimed to be the Way, the Truth and the Life. Yet such revelation always needs to be articulated and mediated, not only through the written word (in books and book learning), but also and most essentially through a person.

Who would that person be for the searching and disillusioned young Augustine? It turned out to be Bishop Ambrose of Milan, who sat day after day in his cathedral teaching the Scriptures. In Augustine he was to have a captive audience. Ambrose was the right man in the right place at the right time. As Augustine was to relate some years later to a friend, 'At that time, there was no one more open to being taught than I was.'

THE PERSON, THE PLACE AND THE TIME

'There is a tide in the affairs of men,' as Shakespeare wrote in the play *Julius Caesar*, and such was the case in the life of Augustine, when he met up with Bishop Ambrose. Through Ambrose's teaching, Monica's son was to discover how very different the claims of the Christian faith were from what he had supposed them to be. It is often the case. The 'faith' that many people are rejecting bears little or no resemblance to the authentic faith of Jesus Christ. Rather, it has been distorted beyond recognition and deserves to be rejected. The problem for the Church in every age is to find a sufficient supply of men and women who know the content of the Christian faith and who are able to communicate it in user-friendly language and in a manner that is accessible to a particular generation and culture. The content and style of Bishop Ambrose's preaching and teaching were certainly very different from the kind of thing Augustine might have overheard back in the days of his youth in provincial North Africa. The person of Ambrose, the place and the special time in Augustine's life all fortuitously converged at a period of deep disillusionment, both with his profession as a teacher and with the exaggerated and phoney claims of the Manichees. 'Through all his wanderings,' writes Henry Chadwick, 'Augustine discerned the watchful hand of an unseen guardian, whose protection had been invoked upon him by Monica when as a baby he was made a catechumen. Decisions made with no element of Christian motive, without any questing for God or truth, brought him to where his Maker wanted him to be.'[10]

Compelled to resign his post as professor of rhetoric because of ill health, displaying symptoms of what we would understand today to be a kind of psychological breakdown, Augustine for the first time experienced unoccupied 'space' in his life, into which the 'hound of heaven' would break. So it was that Augustine's breakdown afforded the opportunity for God to break through.

It was at that point in the summer of AD 386, while he was resting in the garden under the shade of a tree, that Augustine encountered Christ through the words of Scripture. 'Pick up and read' were the words he heard, and as he opened the Scriptures at Paul's Epistle to the Romans, the person of Christ became a reality and a living presence. Until that point Augustine had explored philosophy and religion purely through the mind, seeking union with his Creator by speculation and DIY moral and spiritual purification. All these had collapsed into dust and ashes. It was only when speculation of the mind was met by revelation in a person – an encounter with the living Christ – that the Christian faith became a reality for Augustine.

After this intensely religious experience, Augustine retreated to a friend's villa at Cassiciacum, near Lake Como, together with Monica, Adeodatus and some other friends and students, where he remained throughout the autumn and winter and into the spring of AD 387. Augustine returned to Milan, however, for an intensive Lent course, conducted personally by Bishop Ambrose, in preparation for his baptism at the Dawn Mass of Easter Day on 25 April.

HOMEWARD BOUND

In all his heart-searching 'research', despite his lengthy travels from far-off Thagaste to Carthage, Rome and Milan, Augustine had never found his true self. Like the perpetual restless traveller or tourist, Augustine had supposed that relocation would give him a new start and the opportunity to 'discover himself'. He had always been looking at externals, however, not realizing that our real pilgrimages are always pilgrimages of the heart – journeys of the inner life. When he realized his mistake, he wrote this prayer from the heart:

> Behold you, O God, were within me and I outside; and I sought you outside ... You were with me, and I was not with you. You called and cried to me and broke open my deafness; and you sent forth your beams and shone upon me and chased away my blindness; you breathed fragrance upon me, and I drew in my breath and now I do pant for you: I tasted you and now hunger and thirst for you; you touched me, and I have burned for you.[11]

Augustine decided to return to Africa, to travel back home to the much despised and provincial Thagaste. Now that God was within him, anywhere – even Thagaste – could be a resting place for that restless heart. On the long journey home, however, his mother Monica died of a fever in the port of Ostia while the little party was waiting for a ship to take them to Carthage. As she lay dying, she told Augustine that her lifelong prayer for his conversion had been answered beyond her wildest hopes and therefore she had nothing left to live for.

They were scarcely back home in Thagaste when Augustine's son also died. It is perhaps puzzling that we are given no details concerning the cause or occasion of the death of Adeodatus. Even more significant, perhaps, is the fact that Augustine makes no reference whatever to his own personal grief or sense of bereavement at the loss of his teenage son. It is hard to square all this with the passionate Augustine who, in earlier parts of his spiritual autobiography, spills considerable amounts of ink grieving for a friend who died when Augustine was the age of Adeodatus. It is even more bewildering when we compare this silence with the profound grief Augustine expresses on the death of his mother just a short time before.

What is all this about? Could it be that since becoming a Christian, Augustine was learning to set personal bereavement in the fuller context of the resurrection hope of eternal life? Could it be that, not unlike St Paul, Augustine saw little or no advantage to be gained by remaining in this world longer than necessary? Many people today simply do not know what to do with death and bereavement – they do not know how to talk about death or how to respond to it. Such a generation is light years removed from the Christian mindset of the early centuries, when martyrdom was synonymous with Christian witness. This is not the only area in which Augustine would have had just as much difficulty in relating to our outlook as we have in relating to the Christian perspective of his day. Our attitude to death today is more bound up with the cultural conditioning of post-Enlightenment times than it is with the core faith of Christianity, centred on the hope of resurrection to eternal life. This may not go all the way in explaining

Augustine's strange silence over the death of his son, but it may at least help us to see that our own cultural packaging of Christianity in the West is not the last word on this matter – nor, indeed, on many others. In one of his late sermons, Augustine said of the Christian martyrs, 'They really loved this life; yet they weighed it up. They thought of how much they should love the things eternal, if they were capable of so much love for things that pass away.'[12]

At almost exactly the same time as Adeodatus died, Nebridius – one of Augustine's long-standing friends – also died. With the death of his mother, his son and one of his closest friends, Augustine's life was clearly emptying out, and he was travelling more lightly than he had previously done. What should he do next? Augustine had intended to settle down to a life of prayer with his little lay community of the Servants of God on his return to Thagaste. From his earliest years, Augustine was intuitively drawn to life in some kind of community of friends and an extended family. At first it seemed that his ideal would be realized back in Thagaste. However, it soon becomes evident that the restless heart was once again restless. Thagaste, and all that it had come to stand for, was indeed a geographical signpost on his long spiritual journey, but it was certainly not the finishing post.

So it was that, just two years after the death of his son, Augustine found himself in the cathedral at Hippo, listening to the bishop calling for the ordination of another priest to help him. As sometimes happened in those days, Augustine was compelled by the congregation to come to the feet of the bishop to be ordained, in what is sometimes called 'ordination by acclamation' – a polite theological turn of phrase for religious hijacking, perhaps! Four years later, a similar scene was played out when the Bishop of Hippo called for a bishop coadjutor, and once again Augustine was frogmarched forward, to be ordained a bishop in the Church of God. It was almost as though God had taken Augustine by the scruff of his neck at this point in his spiritual journey. The words addressed by Jesus to Peter after the resurrection could well apply to Augustine at this moment in his life: 'When you were younger, you used to fasten your own belt and to go wherever you wished. But when you grow old, you will stretch out your hands, and someone else will fasten a belt around you and take you where you do not wish to go' (John 21:18).

THE LONG STRETCH

For the next thirty-five years, Augustine served the Church of God as a bishop, as a writer and theologian, and as a protagonist for Christian orthodoxy. His writings were known throughout huge areas of the ancient world and, together with his correspondence with friends and foes alike, impacted the thinking of Christianity powerfully and decisively for centuries to come.

Five years after his ordination to the episcopate, he completed his *Confessions,* tracing in great detail the various stages of his spiritual journey from head to heart and from heart to will. For a record of the last chapters of Augustine's life, however, we have to rely on his extensive theological writings, his sermons, and his letters.[13] We also have the first biography of our saint, written by Possidius shortly after Augustine's death. The thirty-five years of his episcopate were spent in great controversy, as he wrestled with the paradox of grace. Indeed, Augustine is sometimes known as the Doctor of Grace. This name offers an important insight into his life: at one level he had clearly been searching for God, but at another level he had eventually been overwhelmed by a God who had gone out of his way to search out, to find and finally to capture the heart and soul of Augustine.

Towards the close of his life, the disintegration of the Roman Empire became all too apparent as the Goths and Vandals ransacked their way across Roman territories and finally entered Rome itself in AD 410. Under the leadership of Alaric, the Goths attacked the great city, burning and destroying large parts of it. By the time of Augustine's death, large parts of the Church in North Africa had also been totally destroyed, its bishops and clergy martyred and much of his lifetime's work obliterated.

On 28 August AD 430, aged seventy-five, Augustine died, having followed the promptings of the fire in his heart and mind for over forty years since his baptism in Milan on Easter Day, AD 387.

ONE

Setting Out on the Journey

> Thither we make our way, still as
> pilgrims, not yet at rest; still on the
> road, not yet home; still aiming at
> it, not yet attaining it.
>
> *Augustine, Sermon 103*

ORIGINS AND DESTINATIONS

Setting out on any new journey is necessarily an adventure into the unknown. As Augustine probably knew only too well, no journey ever quite turns out to be what we had in mind at the outset. Not only are all journeys full of surprises, but they also occasionally demand a radical change of plan in the light of unexpected events – a mechanical breakdown, perhaps, or road diversions, or the discovery that your map is out of date. Flexibility and a capacity to adapt are the keys to happy and successful travelling. Of course we should also take along any relevant guidebooks, and maps and compass bearings for they also have a part to play in the adventure. It is sometimes helpful to have a guide on board who knows the route, but even the best navigators must be flexible and capable of adapting plans if the need arises.

Life, viewed as a journey, demands the same flexibility and adaptability at every turn in the road. John Henry Newman wrote, 'In a higher world it is otherwise, but here below, to live is to change and to be perfect is to have changed often.'[1] That comment summarizes the whole human story, for it is a story of growth, development and change in our individual lives, as well as in the whole of creation. What point have we reached – collectively, today – in this story of change? Before we start out on our journey of spiritual growth, it may be helpful to think about the way our perception of the world, of ourselves and of God is coloured by that point in history (and in our own personal story) at which we currently find ourselves.

After the decades of revolution which swept across Europe at the close of the eighteenth century, and especially after the massive shift in the cultural mindset associated with the French Revolution and the American War of Independence, the Western worldview was loosened from its moorings and underwent a huge ideological change. From a view of the universe which had been somewhat static and rigid, suddenly everything was in a state of flux. The idea of creation as 'the finished product' was replaced with a different theory which saw it as more of an ongoing process. The rigid certainties enshrined in the scientific dogmatism of the eighteenth century (mirrored by similar 'certainties' associated with the evangelical revival of that same century) suddenly found themselves contending with a much more fluid understanding of an evolving, constantly changing universe. This was accompanied by a new understanding of personality and the changing place of humanity within that ongoing creation process. The old, inflexible formulae no longer fitted the discoveries of new and unprejudiced research on many fronts.

This was largely brought about by the new sciences of geology, biology and the natural sciences (and, later in the nineteenth century, psychology). As well as the new understanding of the universe as a place of constant change, the work of geologists such as Gosse and Lyell, who wrote *Principles of Geology* in 1830, showed that the earth was far older in its origins than had ever been imagined. This was followed by the work of Darwin, who charted a vast map of an ever-evolving creation in which it was possible to trace both continuity and discontinuity. The picture which emerged was of a universe full of surprises, an ongoing story, past, present and future. This idea of evolution through change profoundly disturbed the foundations of Western thought, yet it also resonated with Paul's dynamic picture of creation in his Epistle to the Romans: 'We know that the whole creation has been groaning in labour pains until now; and not only the creation, but we ourselves, who have the first fruits of the Spirit, groan inwardly while we wait for adoption, the redemption of our bodies' (Romans 8:22–3).

John Henry Newman, who was an Anglican priest before he became a Roman Catholic, and whose life almost spanned the entire nineteenth century, wrestled with this new world-view, applying the theories of development and change to his own disciplines of theology and spirituality. How could he hold together the 'faith once delivered to the saints' with an evolving and inevitably changing tradition? What place did change have in an evolving order of things? Thus Newman's theology mirrored the dynamic discoveries of Darwin and others in the realm of biology. Darwin's *Origin of Species,* for example, was published at much the same time as Newman was wrestling with his theology of organic development and its relation to change. Darwin's view of the creation of the universe traced our development through change and adaptation:

far from the universe being created in seven days as a finished product, he claimed, the human story began long ago in the dust of the universe and would continue to develop and change. Creation is not a finished product, handed to us on a plate by the Creator. It is a continuing process, in which we are invited by the Creator to give a hand, to complete together the work which God first planned. You might even say that in the theology of the New Testament, the 'new creation' in Christ is envisaged as a joint enterprise.

Perhaps some words from Isaiah 42, properly translated, will give us a better view of the ongoing nature of creation, in contrast to the view that we find in Genesis, where creation is seen as a completed product. I say 'properly translated', because most translations of these verses use the past tense, rather than the continuous present as given in the original Hebrew. The NRSV, for example, reads, 'Thus says God, the Lord, who created the heavens and stretched them out . . .' A more accurate translation would be, 'Thus says God, the Lord, who is creating the heavens and stretching them out; who is spreading the earth and what comes from it; who is giving breath to the people upon it and spirit to those who are walking in it' (Isaiah 42:5). Surely this is a far more dynamic and exciting view of creation – and, incidentally, a view much more in keeping with contemporary discoveries in astrophysics and other modern scientific theories concerning the nature of an emerging universe.

Cardinal Newman struggled to hold together a 'once-for-all' act of creation with his understanding of development through change. Eventually he resorted to the analogy of the acorn and the oak tree. He contended that there is within the acorn all the latent potential to develop into an oak tree, and the changes through which that development passes are all in accordance with the ultimate image of a fully grown oak.

Of course, these insights carry with them all kinds of disturbing and challenging consequences when we come to apply them to our own spiritual growth, our emotional development and our personal relationships, whether with others or with God. There is a sense in which we can never know God or, indeed, another person as they truly are, with the accompanying danger that we will try to fit others into whatever rigid preconception we may have of them. C.S. Lewis writes:

> Not my idea of God, but God. Not my idea of my neighbour, but my neighbour. For don't we often make this mistake as regards people who are still alive – who are with us in the same room? Talking and acting not to the man himself, but to the picture – almost the précis – we've made of him in our minds? And he has to depart from it pretty widely before we even notice the fact. In real life – that's one way it differs from novels – his words and acts are, if we observe closely, hardly ever quite 'in character', that is, in what we call his character . . . My reason for assuming that I do this to other people is the fact that so often I find them obviously doing it to me. We all think we've got one another taped.[2]

It is one thing to do this to other people, but quite another to do it to God. The Bible calls that idolatry, and that is perhaps the deadliest sin of all. Faith is not a matter of bright ideas, least of all of certainties. Discipleship and pilgrimage demand a willingness to press on through the known and into the unknown, letting go of our rigid preconceptions and pet theories in the light of new horizons and unexpected changes.

In Augustine's faith story, both before his baptism as well as throughout his long life, we discern a continuing ability to move both through discontinuity as well as continuity, repeatedly reviewing and revising. In his early days, Augustine clung to the absolute certainties so typical of the Manichees. 'They had claimed', writes Peter Brown, 'to offer absolute certainties, straightforward and unambiguous to any rational man. The "Wisdom" contained in their books described the exact reality of the universe: all a man need do was to act in conformity with his knowledge.'[3] This ability to review constantly attitudes and insights persisted throughout Augustine's life reaching its ultimate expression, when he totally reviewed and rewrote nearly all of his books during the last years of his life in what has come to be known as Augustine's 'Retractions' – a task he was determined to complete before his death.

Maintaining such an attitude, however, will mean that we must always be open to change – to discontinuity as well as continuity, and discontinuity in one's life can be very disconcerting. An open-ended view of life and the world, in which change can always happen, can be disturbing for those who prefer to have everything cut and dried, who like to think they have everything securely 'taped'. In many ways this is the 'calling's snare' of lawyers. Their craft encourages them to build the superstructures of legal systems on the basis of precedent, with the accompanying temptation to believe that 'as it was in the beginning, is now, and ever shall be'. Perhaps it is not incidental that Jesus said, 'Woe to you lawyers'. Yet his remarks are not confined to professional lawyers, but also take in those people who hide behind the security of the letter of the law, afraid to move out and live by the Spirit to which all good laws point.

Not surprisingly, many people found Darwin's thesis – and Newman's theological ideas – deeply disturbing. Such theories appeared to be in direct opposition to the story of creation as related in the book of Genesis. That is not necessarily so, but Newman was adamant that the model of an evolving and changing universe required a shift in theological emphasis. No theology worthy of the name, he argued, could hold at one and the same time to a dynamic model of creation and to a contradictory and static model of salvation and redemption. The view cherished for so long by the churches, which spoke of a deposit of faith 'once delivered to the saints', therefore required a radical rethink. As it happened, growth and development through change was to become the order of the day on every front, not only in the rather rarefied spheres of biology and theology. It was an alarming prospect for many. While constant change may seem like an exciting challenge to the bold and adventurous, such endless fluidity is often seen as a threat by less robust spirits.

The very concept of constant change is immensely threatening to us as human beings. Change means that familiar landmarks are suddenly no longer as secure as we thought. The framework of our lives is no longer as solid as we had believed. A well-documented example is the trauma associated with the biological change of life experienced by both men and women as they reach a certain age. The increasing popularity of cosmetic surgery (amongst those who can afford it) is a particularly striking example of the insecurity associated with a midlife crisis – the time when many people are suddenly afraid of change, of losing their youthful attractiveness, sexual potency or the energy associated with youth. How sad that such people fail to see that each age in life has its own attractiveness and distinctive characteristics: surely each turn in the road would be better welcomed than feared.

Given our general dislike of change, it is little wonder, when everything within us and around us is changing, that we cling to institutions and practices which we hope will never change. Yet even as we are doing this, we are all too painfully aware that the world around us is also constantly subject to the disturbing forces of change. Furthermore, it is not only

43

change, but also the *speed* of change that constitutes such a threat to so many in our world today.

It is also by no means evident that all change is change for the better – and certainly in some cases, especially when we are facing a big change head-on, it clearly seems to be change for the worse. It is not at all difficult to understand why we so often speak with nostalgia of 'the good old days' when everything appeared to be so simple and straightforward. Perhaps, after all, many of us are naturally somewhat conservative (with a small 'c') since we seldom find ourselves comfortable with change; perhaps we are not nearly so radical in our outlook as we would like to think. Nonetheless, change can often be a positive thing. If we meet somebody we have not seen for years and tell them, 'You haven't changed a scrap,' we mean it in a complimentary way. Yet not to have changed over the course of many years would surely indicate an undeveloped personality, even a lack of achievement – which is anything but a compliment! It is one thing to remain childlike at heart, but something else to remain childish in outlook and personality into middle and late life.

Of course, people in their right minds do not want change for change's sake. If we are to change for the better, however, we require knowledge of our ultimate destination. How else can we make positive progress? Suppose, for example, that we are on a journey and are approaching a fork in the road where there are no signposts. If we do not know our ultimate destination, then there is no such thing as a right or wrong turning. We might as well spin a coin, or put the car on autopilot and just take a chance. Destination determines all responsible decision-making.

At a personal level, such decision-making demands a measure of insight, of self-knowledge (both weaknesses and strengths), as we look beyond the next step to some further destination. We need to be able to distinguish between the immediate and the ultimate; between what is urgent and what is of lasting importance; between strategy and tactics. For many women in the Western world, for instance, the freedom to choose between a career and parenting inevitably brings its own crisis. Having the freedom to opt for a career (surely a good development in itself) is one thing. It is quite another, however, to have the mature perspective to consider a different course, in the light of more far-reaching and longer-lasting considerations.

Ad hoc tactics are not at all helpful on long journeys: at some point, strategy and goals need to come into play. Scientists such as Darwin, and archaeologists, with their study of the world's origins and past development, only give us half the story and half the knowledge we shall need if we are to be responsible makers of change and successfully remade by change ourselves. (So often, after all, a little knowledge is a dangerous thing, and a half-truth is little better than an outright lie.) We do not only need to know where we have come from: much more important is the need to know where we are going – our goal and ultimate destination. The study of such things is known as teleology, and ideally should complement all archaeological discoveries. (Teleology, derived from the Greek and defined as 'ends' or 'goals', indicates direction and purpose; archaeology, also derived from the Greek, indicates origins and beginnings. Both are important, and should be held in tension.)

Such knowledge of our ultimate destination becomes even more necessary when we realize that creation is not yet complete, that evolution is still in progress and – the most exciting, yet awesome factor – that at this late stage in the history of our evolution we actually have a hand in fashioning the emerging universe and the nature of our own future humanity. This is clearly evident on so many fronts, not least in the current pioneering work of genetic engineering. Like it or not, the human race is now increasingly capable of shaping its own genetic future. Yet to pursue heedlessly such research, with little sense of direction or ultimate destination, would be morally and spiritually irresponsible. Many of the results of such research might well set the human race on a genetically irreversible course. We do not know. The ethical implications in genetic engineering are massive, and clearly require teamwork between theologians, philosophers and scientists, in order to ensure that restraint towards and respect for the created order are maintained. Scientific research in cloning and genetic engineering must not be handed a moral blank cheque with no limits attached. At such a time and such a turning point in the human story, the need for moral as well as biological direction becomes paramount – a theme we shall be developing in some detail later.

Part of the trauma of change is to be found in its requirement to break with the past, to set out and to let go of all that is familiar. So much of our everyday life is built on habits – good and bad – formed over the years, on precedent and on well-tried ways of doing things. Not surprisingly, therefore, many are reluctant to exchange these comfortable habits for alternative, unfamiliar and as yet untested ways. After all, every human being has begun life and consciousness within the warmth and security of the womb, curled up in the foetal position. At times of pain, danger and suffering we are tempted to revert to this position, because we cannot or will not open up and face the hazards of change in a changing world. Surely part of the trauma of the birth experience, and similarly the experience of dying, is that it demands that we leave the warmth of the familiar for the larger world of the unknown, always beyond us. (It is a familiar turn of phrase on such occasions: 'Sorry, I can't face up to this. It's beyond me.')

Many of us can recall the deep insecurities we felt when we moved from primary school, where perhaps we had become something of a large fish in a small pond, to secondary school, where we had to start all over again as very much the junior in unfamiliar surroundings. I suspect that kind of reluctance to enter into the new and unknown is an experience common to everybody at some point during the journey of growing up. This is quite understandable. There is always a measure of fear attached to the unknown – unless the fear of the unknown can be replaced with a faith and trust in somebody whom we have come to know and love. St John says, 'Perfect love casts out fear . . . whoever fears has not reached perfection in love' (1 John 4:18). And not only love. Fear makes us cling to whatever we have, hands clasped, windows and doors barred against a world we see as hostile and treacherous. The harsh truth, however, is that we cannot grow up unless we can let go and face up to the challenge of development through change, and even through confrontation.

'I was afraid . . . and I hid myself,' says Adam (Genesis 3:10), and so it has been ever since. The Adam within all of us locks us into a primordial fear which refuses to release us into the adventure of growth through change, on the long journey from security (at least, we perceive it as security) to maturity, where we become who we were originally created to be. 'In my end is my beginning,' says T.S. Eliot.[4] If fear dominates that beginning, I cannot reach my true end. The temptation to cling to early security will rob us of ultimate maturity. Adam must be supplanted by Abraham, the man of faith. Eve must be replaced by Sarah, the patron saint of surprises and unexpected changes (it was Sarah, after all, who had a baby at an unlikely age and named him Isaac, which in Hebrew means 'joke' – 'God, you must be joking'). It was Abraham, the father of faith, who first helped the human race to grasp the opportunity for a fresh start, a new beginning based not on fear but on faith – a faith ultimately fulfilled and perfected in Christ, whom St Paul rightly calls the new Adam, or the second Adam.

The primordial fear of the first Adam drives humanity to be territorial and protective, to cling to the known and to be hostile towards change and the challenge of anything 'alien' – even different creeds, colours and cultures. 'Stick to your own kind, one of your own kind,' as the lyrics say in the musical *West Side Story*. It is that same primordial fear which holds us back from the adventures as well as the risks attached to all living and loving. Locked in a fear that refuses to be replaced by faith, we are sorely tempted to revert to that original foetal position – curled up, trapped in the darkness and diminishment of our own making, refusing to come out into the larger world of light and love, of new and enriched life.

Essentially, there are only two alternatives as we come to the various junctions on life's journey: either we revert to a death (or at least diminishment) through fear as in the old Adam, or we convert to faith, love and life in the new Adam. Either we turn and look back (like Lot's wife) to our origins, placing all our hope in the humanism of the first Adam, or we turn and look forward to our true end in the new Adam – Christ, who is both the beginning and the end. Christ offers us a new beginning, based on faith and trust. One thing is certain: there can be no standing still on the road to maturity. St Paul can rightly say, 'As all die in Adam, so all will be made alive in Christ' (1 Corinthians 15:22).

In order to set out on that journey from the old to the new, from the known to the unknown, we shall need to take risks. In the eyes of the world outside, those risks may well be regarded as irresponsible foolishness. Abraham was a very old man, and it would have been entirely reasonable if he had settled down with what he had, rather than throwing it all to the wind and setting out on a journey with no known end. Yet in undertaking that journey Abraham became, in his old age, the founding father of all those who choose to 'walk by faith, not by sight' (2 Corinthians 5:7).

It is often said that faith is a four-letter word spelt R-I-S-K. Undoubtedly, love always involves risk and vulnerability (and there is no life worth calling life which is not expressed in and through love). C.S. Lewis writes:

> To love at all is to be vulnerable. Love anything, and your heart will certainly be wrung and possibly be broken. If you want to make sure of keeping it intact, you must give your heart to no one, not even to an animal. Wrap it carefully round with hobbies and little luxuries; avoid all entanglements; lock it up safe in the casket or coffin of your selfishness. But in that casket – safe, dark, motionless, airless – it will change. It will not be broken; it will become unbreakable, impenetrable, irredeemable. The alternative to tragedy, or at least to the risk of tragedy, is damnation. The only place outside of Heaven where you can be perfectly safe from all the dangers and perturbations of love, is Hell.[5]

FROM DISLOCATION TO RELOCATION

The first steps on this long journey towards maturity, therefore, demand that we set out from our natural habitat, our 'base camp', wherever that might be. To some extent we have all done just that, simply by going through the birth process. Yet as we travel we shall discover that we need to be born again – and again, and again. Like all dislocations, such moves and changes in environment are often traumatic experiences. Not for nothing are we told that bereavement and moving house constitute two of the most stressful experiences anyone can have in time of peace. If and when we have out-grown our first 'home', however, we must move on. We cannot stand still, even at this early point in our journey towards maturity. T.S. Eliot writes:

In order to arrive there,
To arrive where you are, to get from where you are not,
You must go by a way wherein there is no ecstasy.
In order to arrive at what you do not know
You must go by a way which is the way of ignorance.
In order to possess what you do not possess
You must go by the way of dispossession.[6]

This sense of movement and dislocation, giving place to relocation, will become a recurring pattern in our development through change as we move towards maturity. It is as though at every point we need to repeat the antiphon: 'The Lord gave, the Lord has taken away, blessed be the name of the Lord.' Wherever we are, at whatever stage of our development we reach, we need to recall these words: 'Here we have no lasting city' (Hebrews 13:14). To cling to permanence in the here and now will rob us of what is everlasting and eternal in the hereafter. The umbilical cord binding us to our previous environment will always need to be cut, however painfully, as we reach forward and gasp for our first breath in the new place. Frequently at such moments, as at our birth, we catch our breath and are literally 'inspired', breathing in the fresh air of a larger and more bracing world. This experience will happen repeatedly on our long journey of faith – and it may even be coloured by the nature and circumstances of our first birth, for better or worse. Is it an exaggeration to claim that a mother's own maturity in faith and her willingness to let go of all that is within her will be formative in patterns of movement and dislocation in the faith journey of her child? Perhaps, perhaps not.

One thing is quite clear. All kinds of forces are at work within us (biological, physiological, mental and spiritual) as well as around us (sociological and environmental). These inevitably make for a certain kind of restlessness, a 'divine discontent' – a restlessness which can be harnessed by God, to kick-start the next phase of our journey and to motivate us on our explorations into the unknown.

We saw in Augustine's story how he reached a vital turning point in his life when his mother, his teenage son and one of his best friends all died within a short space of time. This emptying out of his life occasioned a new restlessness in Augustine, who was once again driven out in search of a further vocation in God's service. I can clearly remember, after my mother had died, my father had remarried and I had left home, how suddenly I began to go in search of something to fill the vacuum. There is a well-known joke about three clergymen who were asked the question, 'When does life really begin?' The first one said, 'Why, at birth, of course!' The second said, 'No! Further back, at conception.' The third replied, 'Life really begins when the mother-in-law is no longer around, when the dog has died, and when the kids have left home!' Savage humour, perhaps, yet it makes the point that new life – or at least a new chapter in life – can begin when we no longer have those familiar ties of family, possessions or commitments.

Josephine Butler, the nineteenth-century mystic and social reformer, experienced the tragic death of her little daughter, Eva, who fell from the upstairs landing and died at the feet of Josephine and her husband. 'Never can I lose that memory – the fall, the sudden cry, and then the silence!' Josephine wrote in a letter some time later. For a whole year or more, Josephine retreated into herself in a deep depression, until one day a Quaker lady told her: 'You know, you could have many daughters.' From then on, Josephine Butler took prostitutes from Liverpool into her own home, and worked for many years to repeal the pernicious Contagious Diseases Act. It was through the tragedy of her daughter's death that Josephine was able to begin a new life. We must never suppose that God sends such tragedies. Yet one thing becomes increasingly apparent: he can and he does help us to do something constructive and wonderful on the other side of such sadness. As at the first resurrection, new life comes out of death to the old.

What constitutes this 'divine discontent' – a restlessness which is vital if we are to continue to grow, to move, to change, to relocate, all the way from birth to the grave and beyond? Unhealthy restlessness is born of a nature which can never commit or settle down, but healthy restlessness comes from an inner conviction that the best is yet to come, that the 'golden age', far from being buried in the nostalgic dust of the past, is to be found only in the future, in God's future for us. At such moments of restlessness, we are driven to give place to a quiet belief that we must not settle for second best, we must not settle for what we already have. 'Good' is quite different from 'best'. Perhaps, after all, the endemic sickness of the human race lies in the fact that we are homesick for heaven. Like homing pigeons, we are intuitively always seeking the permanence of that city with eternal foundations. In the meantime, we live in tents as squatters – permanently restless, always moving on.

Something of all this was clearly at the root of much of St Augustine's restlessness. In the introduction to the *Confessions*, he tells us of his restlessness, which drove him throughout his long life, in these famous words: 'You have made us for yourself, and our heart is restless until it rests in you.' Although he was born of a devout and holy mother, he could not settle for a second-hand faith, just as he would not settle for life in his provincial home town. It is always painful for believing parents to accept when their children move away from a conventional, inherited faith. Hopefully, however, the children's apparent discarding of their second-hand faith belongs to an ongoing quest to discover a living faith for themselves in later life. Ideally, parents should be concerned only to sow the seed correctly, and not be too anxious about the harvest. It is not an overexaggeration to say that, even later in the journey, we sometimes need to lose our faith in order to move along and discover a stronger faith and love – part of God's divine gift and grace.

For the first thirty-three years of his life, Augustine was certainly moved, dislocated and relocated in many 'tents', many philosophies and religions, before he began to settle down in the full Christian faith of his mother. He moved geographically from Thagaste to Madaura to Carthage and back again to Thagaste. Then he returned to Carthage, now as a teacher rather than a pupil. Finally, the big break came when he took a boat from Carthage to Rome one night and fled his mother's apron strings. Then he travelled on to Milan, to take up his prestigious post as professor of rhetoric.

Augustine tells us how he had grown disillusioned with Carthage. For one thing, the students there were 'beyond control'; their behaviour was 'disgraceful'. They would 'come blustering into the lecture-rooms like a troop of maniacs and upset the orderly arrangements, which the master [had] made in the interests of his pupils.'[7] As a student, he says somewhat self-righteously, 'I had refused to take part in this behaviour, but as a teacher I was obliged to endure it in others.' So when the opportunity came, he was all too ready to pull up his tent pegs once again and leave for Rome, where connections in the international network of the literary underworld promised him 'better earnings' and stronger enticements. Alypius, one of Augustine's close friends, had already left to study law in Rome, where he had apparently become 'obsessed with extraordinary cravings for gladiatorial shows'. (It certainly took one obsessive personality to spot another in this case!) So, Augustine went to Rome to join his friend.

What about Monica, Augustine's overpossessive mother, and her relationship with her overdependent son? She must somehow be left behind so that Augustine could break loose again, for his restless heart had certainly not yet found its true home or its ultimate resting place.

> She wept bitterly to see me go and followed me to the water's edge, clinging to me with all her strength in the hope that I would either come home or take her with me. I deceived her with the excuse that I had a friend whom I did not want to leave until the wind rose and his ship could sail. It was a lie, told to my own mother – and to such a mother, too![8]

Monica, however, knew her son and was not deceived. Both her love and intuition told her what she could scarcely bear to know. 'She would not go home with me and it was all I could do,' Augustine recalls, 'to persuade her to stay that night in a shrine dedicated to St Cyprian, not far from the ship. During the night, secretly, I sailed away, leaving her alone to her tears and her prayers ... The wind blew and filled our sails, and the shore disappeared from sight.'[9] Perhaps on that occasion, as on so many similar occasions of wrenching departure and letting go, it was the wind of the Spirit that came to Augustine's aid, although he was not capable of recognizing it at the time. In any event, Monica returned home and Augustine, her restless son, travelled on to Rome.

All loving in this life will involve the pain of letting go, if we are to move on and grow, and if we are to allow others to move on and grow. By clinging to security we can be robbed of ultimate maturity. Fleeing the nest can be a painful, even cruel experience, yet such a relocation is essential if we are to develop and grow up in the unique way intended for us. When parents cling to their children, they are in serious danger of destroying or maiming their cherished offspring. For me this idea of letting go is expressed most poignantly in Titian's remarkable painting *Nolle me tangere,* featuring the scene in the Garden of the Resurrection on the first Easter Day when Mary Magdalene recognizes her beloved Jesus and reaches out to grasp him. 'Do not hold on to me,' says Jesus, 'because I have not yet ascended to the Father.' It is as though Jesus is saying, 'Our relationship has changed. We are going to know and love one another in a new and different way – possibly an even more wonderful way. So do not cling on to me or to our past relationship – that must die. Rather, let go and move on into a new and even deeper relationship, which no longer relies on physical proximity, but on spiritual depth' (see John 20:11–17).

Augustine certainly needed to move on and relocate, to grow from that break with the past. His geographical relocations, however, were as nothing compared with his constant and recurring movements from one philosophy to another, as he shopped around the religious options which abounded in the disintegrating empire. The Christianity of the fourth century would have been presented to the young Augustine as a form of 'True Wisdom'.[10] That would have appealed immensely to his intellectual brilliance and arrogance. For Augustine at that time, discipleship was essentially the way of enlightenment, but it was an enlightenment largely confined to the mind.

Not surprisingly, the youthful and restless Augustine was ready prey for the Manichaean missionaries who believed that they had received direct revelation concerning the true nature of God. Carthage had been overrun with such missionaries during Augustine's time there, and he was taken in for quite a while by their dualistic philosophy, which encouraged a schizoid view of the universe. On arriving in Italy, however, Augustine became disenchanted with this latest philosophical fad. That dissatisfaction prompted him to sit at the back of the cathedral in Milan and listen (at first somewhat reluctantly) to the teaching of Bishop Ambrose.

When Augustine reflected on all this in later years, he was not ashamed to see the many shifts in his life as playing a vital part in his overall pilgrimage and discipleship. He saw both his physical and ideological movements as illustrative of God at work in his inner self, prompting him and moving him on at each point in the journey. Throughout the early years of his life, as a young man with a brilliant intellect, Augustine's search was primarily for enlightenment of the mind. He came very slowly to realize that his restlessness was more deeply seated in his heart, his desires, his will and the driving forces of his whole being – but before such realization came, his explorations were largely confined to the intellect, and kept at a safe distance from his rather confused moral life. His belief was still a long way from overtaking his behaviour.

THE GAMES PEOPLE PLAY

Throughout those years of searching, Augustine was in a sense playing games. It is not only children who play games! We all play games of a sort throughout our lives, replicating the games we played in all innocence as children. We play games with God, just as much as we play games of deception with others and even ourselves, pretending that we are searching for him when all the time, like the first Adam, we are really hiding from him – hiding behind the armour-plating of self-protection, afraid to open up to the invasion of love, truth and beauty.

We all have our pet escape devices, whether it be shopping, drinking, comfort eating, erotomania, overwork, or whatever. In the end, however, these hiding games all fail to satisfy that inner longing which is essentially God-shaped and God-driven. In the fourteenth century, the English mystic Richard Rolle wrote these words, which are as true today as they were then: 'Since the human soul is capable of receiving God alone, nothing less than God can fill it; which explains why lovers of earthly things are never satisfied.'[11]

Of course they are not satisfied! We should not be surprised, in a godless age like our own, that greed in all its forms will always come to the forefront. We are looking in the wrong places, seeking a fulfilment which can never be satisfied. Perhaps, however, a certain kind of restlessness (especially among young people) and a drive to try everything is not quite so spiritually sick as a culture that is willing to settle for second best – 1.4 children and a mortgage for life! What many contemporary protesters are saying, just as Augustine and Francis and many other saints have said through the ages, is something like this: 'There just has to be more to life. We are looking for a life worth living, and until we find it we will always be subversive, irresponsible and all the other "negative" things we are so often accused of being.'

The appeal of the beyond is rendered impotent in the face of those who are too easily pleased and who constantly appeal to that dangerous half-truth, 'A bird in the hand is worth two in the bush'. The real challenge is to let go of the former in faith and to hope that the latter are closer at hand and easier to grasp than we might have thought! Until our hands are empty, however, we are simply not open enough to be able to receive the better gift that God is waiting to give us. A proper discontentedness will often motivate genuine exploration, a reaching out from the good to the better and eventually, after long travels, the replacement of the better for the very best of all. The discipline of discipleship and pilgrimage would constantly caution us against being too easily and too quickly satisfied. C.S. Lewis writes:

> It would seem that our Lord finds our desires, not too strong, but too weak. We are half-hearted creatures, fooling about with drink and sex and ambition when infinite joy is offered us, like an ignorant child who wants to go on making mud pies in a slum because he cannot imagine what is meant by the offer of a holiday at the seaside. We are far too easily pleased.[12]

Yes, our prevailing human problem is that we are too easily and too quickly pleased.

It is as though God teases us with flashes of reality, but refuses to give us the substance beyond the symbols and experiences in which those flashes are momentarily packaged. Yet we need to know in the deepest core of our being, in our innermost self, that the truth, beauty, goodness or joy do not just belong to the experiences in which they are packaged or through which they come to us. As Martin Luther said, 'Grace is the experience of being delivered from experience!' C.S. Lewis comments:

> These things, the beauty, the memory of our own past – are good images of what we really desire; but if they are mistaken for the thing itself they turn into dumb idols, breaking the hearts of their worshippers. For they are not the thing itself; they are only the scent of a flower we have not found, the echo of a tune we have not heard, news from a country we have never yet visited.[13]

Like the children of Israel in the Old Testament, we must be constantly on the move spiritually, and sometimes physically – led on by the 'carrots' of truth, beauty and goodness which we experience in our lives, but which will always prove to be elusive and cannot be possessed in any packaging bearing this world's labels. You can find truth, beauty, goodness and joy in all sorts of nooks and crannies in this world, but they are ultimately not of this world and are not intended to be hoarded or possessed on our own terms. The flashes we see of them are the motivation, the carrot, to keep pilgrim 'donkeys' such as you, me and Augustine on the move. It is not a comfortable or predictable life. In the book of Numbers we find a prototype of all spiritual journeys in the story of the Israelites, moving from the bondage of Egypt through the desert to freedom in the land of promise. Whenever the cloud of God's presence settled over the tabernacle, the children of Israel would pitch their tents and settle down for a while too. 'Whether it was two days, or a month, or a longer time, that the cloud continued over the tabernacle, resting upon it, the Israelites would remain in camp and would not set out; but when it lifted they would set out' (Numbers 9:22). Such is the problematic and unsettling lifestyle of all true pilgrims and disciples.

It seems as though God will simply not let us settle down or make the mistake of substituting a resting place or staging post for our ultimate home. He has provided something better, but the trouble is that – unless we respond to this disturbing and moving Spirit within us all – we are always in danger of settling for what we have, for what we feel is comfortable, for what is, in truth, second best. C.S. Lewis is right: 'We are far too easily pleased.'

That journey is just as much an inner journey of the Spirit at work in us as it is an outward journey. The Spirit may well begin, as with Augustine, by enlightening our minds, but the journey does not end there. The inner journey moves from enlightening the mind to warming the heart, and ultimately to firing the will. Real change has to come from within, and we have to desire it. We sometimes make the mistake of supposing that if we move house, or move the furniture around, or take a holiday abroad, we shall somehow be changed for the better. A change of scenery, however, cannot bring about any real change: it does not change *us* in any way. The perennial difficulty is that we take *ourselves* with us wherever we go. Not surprisingly, we are the heaviest piece of baggage! The unchanged pilgrim would turn even paradise into a living hell.

At the age of thirty-three, when Augustine had completed the first stage of his long journey, he finally realized that he had been looking in all the wrong places for the conversion of the heart he so desired. These words from the *Confessions* are worth repeating:

> Behold you, O God, were within me and I outside; and I sought you outside … You were with me, and I was not with you. You called and cried to me and broke open my deafness; and you sent forth your beams and shone upon me and chased away my blindness; you breathed fragrance upon me, and I drew in my breath and now I do pant for you: I tasted you and now hunger and thirst for you; you touched me, and I have burned for your peace.[14]

With the benefit of hindsight, Augustine came to understand (perhaps rather late in the day) that during all those years of relocation and travel, he had not in fact been seeking God. Rather, God had been searching for him while he, like Adam, had been hiding. God really is the 'Hound of Heaven', as the poet Francis Thompson called him, pursuing us through the corridors of time and the labyrinths of life like a hound in pursuit of its prey. Only slowly do we come to realize that St John hits the nail right on the head when he says, 'In this is love, not that we loved God, but that he loved us'

(1 John 4:10). God loved us from the beginning and before, he loved us while we were still in our mother's womb, and always and for ever with a love that will not let us go.

Let us therefore not make the mistake of being too sure that we are looking for God, because in most cases it is just the reverse. God persistently looks for us, yet we persist in hiding from him, using all kinds of manipulative devices of mind and heart. C.S. Lewis amusingly points out how very ridiculous it is to talk of the mouse looking for the cat: on the contrary, 'The cat is looking for the mouse and the mouse had better look out!'

Christian revelation tells us something even more wonderful about this God who seeks us so persistently. The psalmist says with great insight: 'O LORD, you have searched me and known me . . . You search out my path and my lying down, and are acquainted with all my ways' (Psalm 139:1, 3). God knows what we are like, what we are going through. The gospel proclaims the good news, the best news of all: that God in his great love for us has himself undergone dislocation and relocation, in the incarnation of his love revealed to us in his Son, Jesus Christ. Love – real love – is always willing to put itself out, to go out of its way, if need be, all the way from heaven to earth and hell and back again, so that wherever we are in life's journey, God in Christ through his Holy Spirit can meet us and bring us home, just as he met those two bewildered disciples on the road to Emmaus. He meets us wherever we are, even in hell – which is why we affirm in the words of the Creed that 'he descended into hell'.

From our knee-high point of view, of course, it can often seem that this God of ours is mischievously elusive and that so much of our searching is in vain. We are not helped when the Church gives the impression that unless we can accept all the items in the Creed in one mouthful, we are not Christians, or that if we have not jumped through all the right hoops in the right order, we are not the real thing. Perhaps we are not – but we are certainly disciples who are seeking the truth, motivated by a deeply divine discontent with the way things are. If we are truly searching for that ultimate and lasting Way, that Truth and that Life, it could surely be said of us, as it was said of the scribe in the Gospels, that we are 'not far from the kingdom of God' (Mark 12:34).

So we can pray, if we have the courage, 'Batter my heart, three-personed God,' as the poet John Donne, Dean of St Paul's, prayed so passionately. True prayer of the heart must always be fired by our deepest passions and desires. God battered and warmed the heart of John Wesley one night in Aldersgate. He battered Paul's heart on the Damascus road. He battered Augustine's heart on that hot afternoon in a garden just outside Milan. Yet it does not always require anything quite so dramatic to move us on and relocate us at a point further along the road. Sometimes all it needs is for God to catch us off our guard one day, to get us to unbolt the door to our hearts momentarily, and then he has his foot in the door. After that there can be no turning back – we are on the move again.

A few years after I had been ordained back in the 1960s, I underwent a mercifully short period of depression, bordering perilously on a total breakdown. A wise friend suggested that I take a time of complete rest, followed by a period spent in retreat at a monastery. I duly went to Nashdom Abbey, an Anglican Benedictine community. One day after lunch, I had fallen asleep in a chair in my little monastery cell. I woke with a start, bursting into inexplicable tears. Something prompted me to reach for my Bible, which fell open at chapter six of St John's Gospel. The words sprang off the page, as though they had been written just for me, at just that moment: 'Lord, to whom can we go? You have the words of eternal life' (John 6:68). Suddenly I knew I was no longer alone in that room. There was Another with me, heralding the flicker of a flame of renewal and new life – a moment of recognition, if you like. Yes, most certainly, after that there could be no turning back. I was literally on the move again.

QUESTIONS FOR FURTHER REFLECTION

Prayer of St Augustine

Father,
I am seeking:
I am hesitant and uncertain,
But will you, O God,
Watch over each step of mine
And guide me.

Confessions, 11.17

For personal reflection

1. 'To live is to change and to be perfect is to have changed often' (see page 38). What do you see as the principal changes in your life so far? Plot a graph, or draw a time line, of the main changes on a practical or geographical level (leaving school, meeting someone who had a great influence on you, a death, holiday, car accident, falling in love, reading a particular book). How did the external changes influence your mental or spiritual development? Were the changes welcome, or painful? Did your understanding of what happened change over time? Do you see it now as you saw it then? How did God's hand and your

own decisions interact? (Keep this time line, as you will be adding to it later.)

2. How have you experienced the biological changes of life (see page 43), such as puberty, parenthood, acceptance of singleness, middle years, declining faculties? Write down any emotions attached to these – fear, pride, excitement, contentment – at the relevant point on your time line.

3. Think of when you last met someone you had not seen for years (see page 44), perhaps at a school reunion or a family funeral. How did you experience change in others, and how did you cope with their perception of change in you?

4. What is your understanding of your ultimate destination (see page 44)? How does this impact on your decision-making, and is there any further way you feel it should? Analyse your life as objectively as you can to see what it says about your ultimate values: are you comfortable with the results? (Keep notes, as we will be working on this material in a later chapter.)

5. Do you know what your pet escape devices are (see page 57)? Common ones are work, shyness, frenetic activity (often very worthy), drink, and blaming others. Yours may be golf, socializing with friends, shopping or travelling. Are you comfortable about what you have written, or do you need to challenge these points?

For group discussion

1. Look at the story of Paul's conversion, first in Acts 9:1–9, and then in Acts 26:9–20. Under two columns, either working by yourself or on a flipchart in a group, compare the two accounts. What do the differences tell us about the intention and focus of the narrator in each case? Now

contrast this sudden conversion with Paul's struggle in Romans 7:15–24. Do you identify more closely with sudden change or ongoing struggle? Share your testimony of coming to faith and the ongoing challenges you have experienced since then.

2. Work through the questions for personal reflection above, inviting comments and contributions from the group. Allow each person to decide what they are prepared to share – you may, for example, prefer to discuss principles rather than specific details. Indeed, questions of this personal nature will make some people very communicative, and they should be encouraged to be selective in their comments so that everyone has an opportunity to participate.

3. What impact do you think the speed of change (see page 44) has on a sociological level?

4. How does faith cast out the fear of change? 'Either we revert . . . or we convert . . .' (see page 48). What does this mean in practice for us today?

5. Do you agree or disagree with the comments on genetic engineering on page 46? What guidelines would you suggest for future research?

Bible passage for meditation

When you have thought about the content of this passage, try to relax in the truth it contains and absorb it into your heart, your feelings and your will. Allow some time of silence, or perhaps reflective music, for this. It may be helpful to look at your time line first, then hold your life in your mind, so to speak, as you meditate on God's hand in your life.

Philippians 2:12–13

Therefore, my beloved, just as you have always obeyed me . . . work out your own salvation with fear and trembling; for it is God who is at work in you, enabling you both to will and to work for his good pleasure.

TWO

Pursuing Our Heart's Desire

> Thou gavest them their heart's
> desires:
> And sent leanness withal into
> their souls.
>
> *Psalm 106:15 (Coverdale)*

Now don't set your heart on it!' This is a caution born of past disappointments, but such advice frequently goes unheeded. Our experience should teach us, if we were willing to profit from such wisdom, not only that we seldom achieve our heart's desires, but that even when we do they often fail to satisfy us, leading ultimately to deep disappointment and disillusionment.

Nonetheless, longing and the desires of the heart are written into our human make-up, firing our ambitions, infusing our energies, stretching us and preparing us to go after something or somebody 'at all costs'. Singleness of mind alone will never do the trick; our objectives are seldom achieved simply in the cold light of reason. We need to go further and claim that the first step towards true and lasting fulfilment is to want something badly enough and to be willing to sacrifice all else, if necessary, in order to attain it. It is that kind of singleness of mind (or 'purity of heart' in the language of the New Testament) for which Jesus is appealing as he entices us in the parables to pursue his kingdom. 'The kingdom of heaven,' says Jesus, 'is like treasure hidden in a field, which someone found and hid; then in his joy he goes and sells all that he has and buys that field. Again, the kingdom of heaven is like a merchant in search of fine pearls; on finding one pearl of great value, he went and sold all that he had and bought it' (Matthew 13:44–6).

There is no chance of movement, growth or a lasting change of heart until we have distilled and discerned our full-blooded desires and longings – what the New Testament calls our 'treasures'. Once we discover where our treasures are lodged, then we shall also know where our heart resides – what we have 'set our heart on'. The desires of the heart define the geography and location of the will. Jesus says, 'Where your treasure is, there your heart will be also' (Matthew 6:21).

The inner life of the spirit does not take place simply in the mind: it is never enough to have religion exclusively on the brain! What is conceived in the mind needs to connect with the desires of the heart, if they are ever to be accomplished by the will. Such actions speak louder than words and can radically affect the way we live our lives, the way we define our priorities and focus our objectives. In the same way, the life of faith can take the 'water' of our desires and change it into the full-blooded 'wine' of our God-infused desires, which ultimately cannot be satisfied with anything less than the embrace of God himself, who exceeds all that we could ever desire. It takes the wind of the Spirit to set alight the rational ideas of the mind, to warm the desires of the heart, and to fire the will, redirecting our lives towards God. Christian discipleship should not dampen our desires, but rather redirect them. We need to bring to God what really makes us tick, what really matters to us, even if – in the early stages of our pilgrimage – those desires are attached to the wrong objectives.

St Augustine writes of the desires of the heart:

Give me a man in love; he knows what I mean. Give me one who yearns; give me one who is hungry; give me one far away in the desert, who is thirsty and sighs for the spring of the Eternal country. Give me that sort of man; he knows what I mean. But if I speak to a cold man, he just does not know what I am talking about.[1]

Or consider this poem:

> i was talking to a moth
> the other evening
> and he was trying to break into
> an electric light bulb
> and fry himself on the wires.
>
> 'it is better to be happy
> for a moment
> and be burned up with beauty
> than to live for a long time. . .'
>
> i do not agree with him
> but at the same time i wish
> there was something i wanted
> as badly as he wanted to fry himself.[2]

Unlike some of the religions of the East, authentic Christian spirituality addresses these longings and yearnings of the heart, incorporating them into a warm spirituality. In the

Psalms there are endless references to the heart and its long-ings. In fact, it is not an overstatement to claim that the whole tapestry of the Psalms is interwoven with these threads: the Psalms are a strange mixture of prayers of passionate desires – dark as well as light.

> As a deer longs for flowing streams,
> so my soul longs for you, O God.
>
> Psalm 42:1

> I long for your salvation, O LORD.
>
> Psalm 119:174

> Whom have I in heaven but you?
> And there is nothing on earth that I desire other
> than you.
>
> Psalm 73:25

Spiritual writer Thomas Traherne dedicates a whole poem simply to 'Desire'.

> For giving me desire,
> An eager thirst, a burning, ardent fire,
> A virgin infant flame,
> A love with which into the world I came,
> An inner hidden heavenly love,
> Which in my soul did work and move,
> And ever, ever, me inflame
> With restless longing, heavenly avarice,
> That never could be satisfied,
> That did incessantly a Paradise
> Unknown suggest, and something undescried
> Discern, and bear me to it; be
> Thy name for ever praised by me . . .[3]

By contrast, many writers on spirituality would appear to encourage us to cool our desires rather than to befriend them. These writers do not represent a genuine Christian spirituality: the Judaeo-Christian tradition speaks directly to the longings of the heart. We have frequently been led to suppose that the saints and other notable holy men and women were encouraged to lose any burning desires they possessed in some overwhelming conversion experience. This cold rejection of desire and passion is something of a caricature, however. Such advice was perhaps given to those displaying unhealthy desires bordering on obsession, but even in such cases the answer is not necessarily to be found in 'cooling' those desires. Such passionate people are frequently the raw material of which monks and nuns are made. It is not insignificant that St Francis of Assisi, as a young man, had a passion for clothes – a passion bordering on compulsion – from which he could only be freed by taking up the vow of poverty, donning the simple costume of the Franciscan order and living the life of a friar. That was his particular road to freedom. Far from being 'cooled', his desires and passions were redirected towards God, and he was released to use his energy in a constructive, God-filled way. That was what the religious life, the example of the monasteries and convents, was intended to achieve.

SIGNPOSTS, NOT FINISHING POSTS

Let's pause for a moment and look at what a proper asceticism really means, disentangled from its many perversions and caricatures. There is, certainly, a crying need to exercise detachment from wrong worldly entanglements. This is not because they are always bad in themselves. It may be that the object of our desires is harmless and quite good in itself, but is nevertheless simply not good enough – not good enough to bring us ultimate fulfilment. Thank God that the world is littered with symbols, icons and signposts that indicate the need to journey onwards and so to 'pass through things temporal, that we finally lose not the things eternal'.[4]

An icon is intended to point beyond itself to the glory which is always far past the point to which we have already travelled: it is not intended to be a mirror to look at, but rather a window for us to look through, to the larger world beyond. As we journey through life, the road will be littered with these signs of a greater Presence, since 'the whole earth is full of [God's] glory' (Isaiah 6:3) for those with eyes to see. It is as though God leaves his fingerprints and his 'DNA' all over the universe, frequently in the most unlikely places.

Isaiah, for example, could reasonably expect to discover evidence of the presence and glory of God in the holy place set aside for that purpose, namely the Temple of God. What he most certainly did not expect when he entered the Temple on the momentous day of his vision (described in Isaiah chapter 6) was that, once he had experienced the intimate presence of God in the place where he was, his mission was to go out and uncover, recover and discover that same glory and presence everywhere. That, however, is precisely the nature of both pilgrimage and mission. Mission will inevitably be built into our pilgrimage, as it was for the good Samaritan who, 'while travelling' (Luke 10:33), undertook responsibility for the wounded man. Pilgrimage and mission converge for all of us at some point on the long journey of faith, as we discover for ourselves our own distinctive vocation within the greater purposes of God. We shall look at this process in more detail later on. Note now, however, that Christian pilgrimage should never deteriorate into a self-indulgent search for personal fulfilment. True fulfilment is an unselfconscious – almost incidental – by-product of responding in faith to our distinctive vocation.

Some of the signposts or prompts we will experience on our journey of life will come at times of pain. A heartbreaking love affair, or even an adolescent crush, can serve to break us open, leaving us vulnerable yet encouraged to go on looking, searching, seeking and longing. Other icons and signs are to be found in the visual arts and music, as well as in countless numinous moments as we admire the beauty of a sunset or views of the earth from outer space. These experiences capture our imagination and infuse our desires, continually uprooting us from our apathy and leading us onwards and inwards with an ever-deeper longing.

> Like tides on a crescent sea beach
> When the moon is new and thin,
> Into our heart's high yearnings
> Come welling and surging in
> Come from the mystic ocean
> Whose rim no foot has trod
> Some of us call it longing
> And others call it God.[5]

All icons, if we look at them correctly, point beyond themselves. The very best in this life is intended to tease us and to point us towards that which is even better, which lodges temporarily in all things, yet which ultimately resides beyond all things. 'All true art,' wrote Thomas More, 'points beyond itself to the Creator of creators.' There is always a danger, however, that we will get hung up on these icons and turn them into idols – ends rather than means. It is a constant temptation. The great and recurring caution given by John in his New Testament epistles is a warning to all would-be disciples and pilgrims against the perennial temptation to idolatry: 'Beware of idolatry,' he says repeatedly. Yet we need to remember that such caution is not the prohibition of some killjoy God, but is born of an enlightened self-interest, from a God who desperately desires our ultimate fulfilment in true and lasting joy. We were created for the worship of the one true God and, in the words of the Westminster Catechism, are destined to 'enjoy him for ever'. In the second verse of the poem quoted above, Thomas Traherne distinguishes between what he calls the 'objects', or icons, and the 'sense' of reality which passes through them, dismissing the former as mere 'toys'.

> This soaring, sacred thirst,
> Ambassador of bliss, approached first
> Making a place in me
> That made me apt to prize, and taste, and see;
> For not the objects but the sense
> Doth bliss to souls dispense,
> And make it, Lord, like thee.
> Sense, feeling, taste, complacency, and sight.
> These are the true and real joys,
> The living, flowing, inward, melting, bright,
> And heavenly pleasures; all the rest are toys;
> All which are founded in desire,
> As light in flame, and heat in fire.[6]

So we need to be wary of these idols, which can so often masquerade as icons, for ultimately they will rob their worshippers of lasting enjoyment – failing to produce what they promise. With this image in mind, it is not an exaggeration to say that all sin is misplaced worship and results from allowing ourselves to fall into the trap of worshipping the creation instead of its Creator. As St Paul puts it, 'They exchanged the truth about God for a lie and worshipped and served the creature rather than the Creator' (Romans 1:25). In the words of William Cowper's hymn:

> The dearest idol I have known,
> What ere that idol be.
> O help me tear it from thy throne
> And worship only thee.

SOME CONTEMPORARY IDOLATRIES

For many people, idolatry presents itself as most seductive in the realm of their sexuality, and much that has been paraded as Christian discipleship has suggested that erotic love should be separated from *agape* or platonic love if the virtue of chastity is to be realized. 'Quench the fires,' we are told – suppress this powerful desire. Yet no road to ultimate freedom will be found down the side road of escapism. When people spurn their sexuality and its accompanying desires, they cut themselves off from that vitalizing and creative power which is fired by human sexuality (both biological and psychological). There are no shortcuts to the kind of chastity that brings wholeness.

To hold together both *eros* and *agape* in a mature and loving way demands an awareness that can only come from a proper integration of thinking, feeling and sensing. This kind of knowledge is reflected in the Hebrew verb *yadah*, which implies a form of knowledge that results only from the integration of mind, heart and will – all saying the same thing and all pointing in the same direction. This integration of all the driving forces within us was called 'integral cognition' by one of the great Russian Orthodox philosophers of the nineteenth century, Ivan Kireyevsky (1806–56), who wrote:

> The first condition for the elevation of reason is that man should strive to gather into one indivisible whole all his separate forces, which in the ordinary condition of man are in a state of incompleteness and contradiction; that he should not consider his abstract logical capacity as the only organ for the comprehension of truth; that he should not consider the voice of enraptured feeling uncoordinated with other forces of the spirit as the faultless guide to truth; that he should not consider the promptings of an isolated aesthetic sense, independent of other concepts, as a true

guide to the comprehension of the higher organization of the universe; that he should not consider even the dominant love of his heart, separate from the other demands of the spirit, as the infallible guide to the attainment of the supreme good; but that he should constantly seek in the depth of his soul that inner root of understanding where all the separate forces merge into one living and whole vision of the mind.[7]

Clearly the attainment of such integration and integrity requires discipline, for discipline and discipleship go together and are closely related in many ways. Yet this disciplining of our desires and all the creative forces within us should never become an end in itself, but should be pursued for the sake of the fuller, richer life which Jesus refers to as 'abundant life' (see John 10:10). The resulting integration, by the grace of God, is a special holistic 'knowledge' that enables people to listen to the messages from all the aspects of the self. This is precisely because Christianity is not a spiritual religion, but rather a sacramental and incarnational religion in which the Word – Love – is continuously expressed through the flesh and through matter, rather than seeking to bypass it. Archbishop William Temple was expressing something of this when he described Christianity as the 'most materialistic of all religions'. Jesus is not ashamed to say to his disciples, both then and now, 'This is my body, which is given for you' (Luke 22:19). He does this for much the same reason, and to a similar end, as a bride and groom do when they pledge their love to one another, declaring in the astounding words of the old Book of Common Prayer, 'With my body, I thee worship.' A man and wife must become 'one flesh', and Jesus and his disciples must become the 'body of Christ'.

When Augustine notoriously prayed, 'Lord, make me chaste – but not yet', it meant that chastity for Augustine was still, at that point on his journey, largely an ideal lodged in the mind, rather than what it had yet to become – namely, a deep and consuming desire of the heart and ultimately the overriding, driving force of his will. As he was to discover, however, just as many others have also discovered, progress in this aspect of his discipleship would ultimately only come from grace, and not from 'doing what comes naturally'.

Perhaps a more pernicious contemporary idolatry, certainly for many in the West, is that which results from consumerism and greed. We should understand first that Paul did not say, as he is frequently misquoted, 'Money is the root of all evil'. Instead he said, 'The love of money is a root . . . of evil' (1 Timothy 6:10). We were not made to love things and use people; we were made to love people and to use things in general and money in particular to good ends and for the support of those in need. To worship money or to desire it inordinately results in perverted worship. There is nothing intrinsically wrong with being rich. Whether you are rich or poor, you can still have both right and wrong attitudes to wealth. Too much money, however, like too little of it, can often result in a compulsive desire for more. Then, since money in itself can never fulfil our desires, we can never get enough of it. Like so much of God's creation, money is morally neutral: it all depends what we do with it. For some people money, like sex and alcohol, has taken them over and is driving them from one excess to another, so that in the end they can never be rescued from their compulsions without totally giving them up. Only in such radical 'surgery' will they ever find freedom. In the words of Jesus, 'If your right hand causes you to sin, cut it off and throw it away; it is better for you to lose one of your members than for your whole body to go into hell' (Matthew 5:30). All wrongly directed and unrestrained desires ultimately lead to compulsive behaviour, which in turn brings neither pleasure nor delight to the person concerned, nor to their friends and loved ones who have to live with such self-destructive behaviour.

DETACHMENT AND RELOCATION

There is a phrase used by Jesus in the New Testament which is frequently misunderstood, because it was originally wrongly translated in the King James Version of the Bible – a translation that is still deeply rooted in the collective psyche of the English-speaking world. Jesus did not say, 'In my Father's house are many mansions . . . I go to prepare a place for you' (John 14:2 KJV). The word translated as 'mansions' actually means anything but a mansion. The word in Greek gives us our word 'caravan', and should be translated as nothing more than a staging post, a resting place – at best a motel, nothing as fancy as a hotel! Such staging posts in the Eastern world at the time of Jesus were to be found all along the main trading routes, and were used as places for an overnight stop, for bed and board. They were never regarded as permanent residences, let alone as mansions.

G.K. Chesterton takes up this image when he suggests that for travellers, pilgrims or hikers on a long walk, there is 'a time when the road points to the pub and yet another time when the pub points back to the road.' You have been walking all morning, he says, and as lunchtime approaches you sense that you are being drawn to a pub for refreshment and a rest. In being drawn to the pub, he suggests, it is almost as though the road is actually 'pointing' to it – leading you to that ploughman's lunch and a place to put your feet up for a while by the warmth of a fire. Yet you must not get too comfortable in that pub, because you have not reached your ultimate destination. So it is not long before a kind of restlessness comes over you, even though you might feel a little reluctant to get back on the road, to go out into the bracing air. Yet move on you must, if you are not to give in to the seduction of the immediate comfort of your resting place and miss out on the point of it all – home, a hot bath and a good night's rest after a satisfying day out. Eventually you pull yourself away, in obedience to the impression that now, having temporarily drawn you in, the pub is pointing back to the road.

The complementary dynamic and corrective effects of detachment and relocation hold good in all human relationships, and more especially as we seek to know God, who will always be to some extent unknowable by the mind or constrained by finite concepts and images. For all pilgrims – always on the move, squatting in 'tents' by the roadside – the saying of Jesus represents a constant antiphon as we press on from one glimpse of God's glory to a greater one, and so on until we are ultimately rewarded with nothing less than the vision of God. Jesus says to true disciples, 'A little while, and you will no longer see me, and again a little while, and you will see me' (John 16:16). He also was on a journey back to his Father: 'I go to prepare a place for you ... so that where I am, there you may be also' (John 14:2, 3).

J.J. Balfour wrote:

> Our highest truths are but half-truths.
> Think not to settle down forever in any truth.
> Make use of it as a tent in which to pass a
> summer's night,
> But build no house of it, or it will be your tomb.
> When you first have an inkling of its insufficiency
> And begin to descry a dim counter-truth looming
> up beyond,
> Then weep not, but give thanks
> It is the Lord's voice whispering, 'Take up thy bed
> and walk.'[8]

Pilgrims and disciples are not being asked to be 'cool', to live in a state of indifference or even apathy, an attitude apparently much admired among many young people today. To be indifferent is to be less than human, and excludes any possibility of being touched by the divine. Any ideal that attempts to overcome desire and replace it with cool reason is both inhuman and unattainable. Whenever the Spirit of God touches us, far from being 'cool', we become in every sense 'charismatic'. For the pilgrim, the gentle art of life in the Spirit is to move and be moved, to allow ourselves to be dislocated in order to be relocated further along the path – following in the footsteps of the 'author and perfecter of our faith' (see Hebrews 12:2), who had nowhere to lay his head until he eventually bowed his head and yielded up his spirit on the cross of Calvary. Gregory of Nyssa writes, 'This truly is the vision of God: never to be satisfied in the desire to see him. But one must always, by looking at what he can see, rekindle his desire to see more.'[9]

Spiritual advisers do well to speak of 'the place of detachment' when schooling would-be pilgrims; to speak again and again of being in the world but not of it. Yet they should do this only on the understanding that such detachment results from a compelling need to restrain and redirect our desires and passions. We often speak of doing 'too little, too late'. The pilgrim might well adapt this saying to 'not too much, too soon'. Desire and detachment need to interact and complement one another as the driving force and the motivating power for long journeys of faith. Like Rome, such journeys are not completed in a day. We need to pace ourselves for the long haul, and our needs and reactions will be different at the various stages along the way.

> Through desires of unquiet love
> The soul can win no repose,
> And through desires of strong love

It loses repose and inner quiet.
So it drowns in sublime Love,
And so it finds its unattainable desire nearby;
For anyone in misery cannot find contentment
Unless desire can be fulfilled;
For desire comes from such a lofty nature,
It cannot be at rest in any small thing.
Love flees, and desire follows hard after,
And never finds a resting place.[10]

REDIRECTING AND RELOCATING OUR DESIRES

As we have seen, one essential rule for the pilgrim in the
Spirit must be a refusal to stand still. We must never clasp a
signpost as though it were the finishing post. The disciples
on the road to Emmaus, we are told, 'stood still, looking sad'
(Luke 24:17). Things had not turned out as they had so desperately wanted them to: 'We had hoped . . .' they tell Jesus,
with eyes cast down (24:21). Their hope had become located
in the past, and they seemed to think that both the present
and the future were therefore hopeless. It is so sad to see
priests, monks and nuns, as well as committed churchgoers,
who have ceased to travel as pilgrims and who have not
changed since the day of their confirmation, ordination or
the taking of life vows. They have not lost their faith, but
they have never found a renewed and living faith. The glow
has gone and the smiles are fewer. They are standing still, and
inevitably they are 'looking sad'.

Even worse than just standing still is the temptation to
stand still and constantly look back at the so-called 'good old
days'. Lot's wife, who stopped and turned to look back, was
promptly turned into a pillar of salt. She atrophied, you might
say – dried up and died. Jesus explicitly tells us that nobody
who 'puts a hand to the plough and looks back is fit for the

kingdom of God' (Luke 9:62). Abraham was always being exhorted by God to 'look up', not back, to focus his gaze on the distant horizon and beyond, to look forward to the land of promise. So it is with all the children of Abraham, the father of faith. They should not be downcast by the present, but should always direct their gaze upwards and beyond the immediate, towards their ultimate destination.

To be healthy is to live fully, wherever you are on the journey of life – to 'act your age'. Every stage of life has its glory, be it childhood, adolescence, young adulthood, middle age or old age. Shakespeare wrote of the seven ages of man – for each age there is an appropriate and healthy characteristic, provided that we are not constantly looking back and refusing to move on and grow up.

> And one man in his time plays many parts,
> His acts being seven ages. At first the infant,
> Mewling and puking in the nurse's arms.
> And then the whining schoolboy, with his satchel,
> And shining morning face, creeping like snail
> Unwillingly to school. And then the lover,
> Sighing like furnace, with a woeful ballad
> Made to his mistress' eyebrow. Then a soldier,
> Full of strange oaths, and bearded like the bard,
> Jealous in honour, sudden and quick in quarrel,
> Seeking the bubble reputation
> Even in the cannon's mouth. And then the justice,
> In fair round belly with good capon lin'd,
> With eyes severe, and beard of formal cut,
> Full of wise saws and modern instances;
> And so he plays his part. The sixth stage shifts
> Into the lean and slipper'd pantaloon,
> With spectacles on nose and pouch on side,
> His youthful hose well sav'd a world too wide
> For his shrunk shank; and his big manly voice,

Turning again towards childish treble, pipes
And whistles in his sound. Last scene of all,
That ends this strange eventful history,
Is second childishness, and mere oblivion,
Sans teeth, sans eyes, sans taste, sans everything.[11]

Healthy development, then, demands that we not only relocate our desires but also redirect them. Desire is the energy force of all our longing and searching, keeping us both moved and moving. St Augustine writes, 'Love cannot be idle. What is it that moves absolutely any man to do evil, if it is not love? Show me a love that is idle and doing nothing. Scandals, adulteries, crimes, murders, every kind of excess, are they not the work of love? Cleanse your love then. Divert into the garden the water that was running down the drain.'[12]

So we need to redirect our desires – even the base desires that can drive us to evil deeds – and reattach them to objects worthy of our heart's desire. Elizabeth Bassett writes, 'Sadly, it seems that this yearning can become misdirected into channels which lead to drugs or drink or other excesses for excitement to assuage the longing when it has not been recognized for what it is.' Sometimes it takes many years for us to realize that we have been chasing wrong or unworthy ends. Sometimes we only realize this when we have achieved all those ends and find that we are still deeply discontented and perhaps disillusioned, and that what looked so promising in prospect has crumbled and gone sour when acquired. It took Augustine over thirty years to arrive at this point. For the first three decades of his life he pursued pleasure, ambition, happiness and wealth, all of which he had achieved by the time he became professor of rhetoric in Milan. Yet he found himself experiencing a deep inner dissatisfaction. Simone Weil comments, 'We do not desire anything else, we possess it, and yet we still desire something. We do not in the least know what it is. We want to get behind beauty, but it is only a surface. It is a sphinx, an enigma, a mystery which is painfully tantalizing.'[13]

In the church of St Augustine in San Gimignano, Italy, there is a famous series of wonderfully preserved frescoes telling the story of Augustine's life. One of them is especially striking. It shows an evidently successful young Augustine, setting out from Rome to go to Milan to take up his new post. This fresco captures the young man's self-assurance, as he stands with his manservant and horse ready to mount. He is well dressed and is clearly setting his feet on the road to a brilliant career. That is by no means the complete story, however. In his later years Augustine looks back on that episode in his long life with insight and ruthless self-analysis. By the time he reached Milan, he tells us in the *Confessions,* he was 'eager for fame and wealth and marriage', but at another level he had come to realize that he was now in his thirties and 'still floundering'. Furthermore, the sycophantic nature of his relationship with the court at Milan sickened his sense of integrity.

His misery was complete, he found, when he had to prepare a speech in praise of the emperor, 'intending that it should include a great many lies which would certainly be applauded by an audience who knew well enough how far from truth they were'. It so happened that he was thinking about the speech as he walked along a street in Milan, when he noticed a beggar who had somehow managed to have his fill of food and drink. The beggar was laughing and joking. The contrast between the contented beggar and Augustine's own inner misery made him turn to his companions and comment ruthlessly on his personal predicament. 'My ambitions had placed a load of misery on my shoulders and the further I carried it the heavier it became.' The beggar appeared to have found a kind of happiness that Augustine felt to be quite beyond his grasp. 'For all my laborious contriving and intri-

cate manoeuvres I was hoping to win the joy of worldly happiness, the very thing which this man had already secured at
the cost of a few pence which he had begged.'

Augustine realized that he was not in his heart of hearts
a rich, successful and notable professor of rhetoric after all –
a step forward in self-knowledge similar to the one made by
the 'rich young ruler' in the New Testament (see Mark 10:17–
22). Douglas Rhymes comments, 'Often we do, in fact, receive
what we really desire, not what we feel we ought to desire,
and the result is that our whole personalities become dwarfed
and stunted.'[14] For all his achievements, Augustine felt himself
impoverished – 'dwarfed and stunted' – and poorer than the
happy beggar he had observed in the street. None of his ambitions, desires or hopes was wrong in themselves. It was just
that they had become attached to objectives which would
never ultimately reward him or fulfil his heart's desire. Like
the 'toys' which Thomas Traherne wrote about, they needed
to be discarded and willingly exchanged for the real thing.
Augustine's desires needed to be redirected and relocated.

BREAKDOWN AND BREAKTHROUGH

How was this to come about, though? Augustine's story of
changed directions is replicated in the stories of many people.
We tend to refer to such experiences now as 'a mid-life crisis'.
Augustine had achieved everything to live with, without yet
discovering anything to live for. The choice of the word 'crisis', which at its Greek root means 'judgement', is a telling
one. Augustine's crisis manifested itself at first in physical
symptoms. During the summer of AD 386 he developed 'a
weakness of the lungs', he 'found breathing difficult', had
pains in his chest, and his 'voice was husky'. He could no
longer 'speak for long at a time'. To say the least of it, this
was a serious condition for an orator and a wordsmith, a

professor who made his living by speaking. These symptoms were accompanied by a general feeling of exhaustion and debilitation. Today we would probably speak of such a condition in terms of having a breakdown.

It is often the case that our times of breakdown are the times when God can break through and at last get a foot in the door – the door which at times of success and strength we keep firmly shut and bolted. These times of breakdown can come in different guises: times when we are laid low by illness; times of grief and bereavement; times when we suffer a big reverse, for example by being made redundant, as a result of which we feel irrelevant or useless. Such a condition is further compounded if we have been especially successful or famous or a notable workaholic, deriving our essential identity from what we do rather than who we are.

Thus Augustine underwent a typical kind of breakdown, at the very peak of his career. At the very moment when all that he had ever desired appeared to be within his grasp, everything fell apart.

Out of the chaos of my doubt
And the chaos of my art
I turn to you inevitably
As the needle to the pole turns...
As the cold brain to the soul
Turns in its uncertainty;

So I turn and long for you;
So I long for you, and turn
To the love that through my chaos
Burns a truth
And lights my path.[15]

As these words by Mervyn Peake describe, so it was for Augustine. That summer proved to be a time of breakthrough as well as breakdown. 'There was a small garden attached to the house where we lodged,' Augustine tells us. 'I now found myself driven by the tumult in my breast to take refuge in this garden, where no one could interrupt that fierce struggle, in which I was my own contestant, until it came to its conclusion.' And indeed it was a struggle: 'I tore my hair and hammered my forehead with my fists . . . I locked my fingers and hugged my knees.' In that garden Augustine 'probed the hidden depths' in his soul. Perhaps we have all been there at some point in our pilgrimage, though we may not describe the occasion with such intensity.

At last Augustine began to acknowledge his 'powerlessness' in those areas of his life that would eventually determine his lasting fulfilment and contentment. Suddenly, he tells us, 'a great storm broke within me, bringing with it a great deluge of tears.' He stood up and left his friend Alypius, who was sitting with him, so that he 'might weep and cry to my heart's content'. He flung himself down 'beneath a fig tree and gave way to the tears.' Then all at once, he 'heard the singsong voice of a child in a nearby house'. This is the most dramatic – and perhaps the most well known – chapter of the *Confessions*. Augustine tells the story vividly.

> Whether it was the voice of a boy or a girl I cannot say, but again and again it repeated the refrain, 'Take it and read, take it and read.' At this I looked up, thinking hard whether there was any kind of game in which children used to chant words like these, but I could not remember ever hearing them before. I stemmed my flood of tears and stood up, telling myself this could only be a divine command to open my book of scripture and read the first passage on which my eyes should fall. For I had heard the story of Antony, and I had remembered how he had happened to go into a church while the gospel was being read

and had taken it as a counsel addressed to himself . . . So I hurried back to the place where Alypius was sitting, for when I stood up to move away I had put down the book containing Paul's Epistles.

Augustine seized the book, opened it, and read the first passage that caught his eye. The passage that spoke to him was from Romans: 'Not in revelling and drunkenness, not in debauchery and licentiousness, not in quarrelling and jealousy. Instead, put on the Lord Jesus Christ' (Romans 13:13). The words were deeply significant, but Augustine's experience that day went further. Jesus Christ made himself known to Augustine that day, not so much through the knowledge of the mind (i.e. 'head knowledge', or *savoir* knowledge as the French would say), but rather through that deeper knowledge of the heart (i.e. *connaître* knowledge, to use the French distinction). Here was a classic case of the words of Scripture being the vehicle for the living Word of healing and salvation. Jesus, God's living Word, was made present through the working of the Holy Spirit – not *in* the words of Scripture, but *through* them. It is not so much what is said but who is saying the words that lends power and authenticity to the words of Scripture.

Such was the most significant turning point in Augustine's journey of faith – the day when, in Augustine's moment of breakdown, God was at last able to break through. To adapt Winston Churchill's words, this was not the end of the story, nor even the beginning of the end, but rather the end of the beginning – perhaps only the end of the first act, if you like. At that moment Carthage, Thagaste and his home back in North Africa must have seemed a long way away to Augustine. He had left home in the vain hope that he could make a new start and become a different person in a different environment. In fact, as we all do, he had taken all the luggage of his old self with him, and until that day of revelation, nothing much had changed. Nevertheless, the events in the garden on that hot summer's afternoon were to prove formative. There was no going back.

Augustine decided to drop his career altogether and to take time out. Vacation time was approaching in any case. A close friend called Verecundus offered Augustine and his household the use of his large country house at Cassiciacum for as long as they cared to stay, and Augustine gratefully accepted. (Verecundus died the following year, having been received into the Christian faith on his deathbed.) As soon as the vacation was over, he notified the authorities in Milan that 'they must find another vendor of words for their students'. He gave two reasons for his resignation: in the first place he was now a Christian and intended to be baptized, and in the second place he was far from well.

Augustine had finally broken loose from the noose of his own making. He was back out on the open road of faith, seeking the redirection and relocation of those early longings and desires which he now realized had brought him to a dead end. It was at that very dead end, however, that God was able to meet him – redirecting him to where the side road rejoined the main road further on, with the offer of free, unearned and amazing grace.

QUESTIONS FOR FURTHER REFLECTION

Prayer of St Augustine

O God of power
bring us back to you:
Show us your mercy and we shall be saved.
Wherever I may turn away from you,
and however beautiful the things I cling to,
my human soul is wedded to sorrow.
Yet beautiful things would not exist
if they did not have their origins in you.
They have both life and death:
once born they live and grow
and come to maturity,
but no sooner do they mature
than they fade and die.
At the very moment of birth
And of reaching out towards existence,
they are hurrying still more swiftly
towards death.
Such is the limit
you have set upon them,
because they are but parts of that reality
which has no existence of itself,
being made up of mere fragments that fade away. . .
My soul must not cling to
the things of creation;
Instead it must sing your praises,
O God, the creator of all things.

For personal reflection

1. 'There is no chance of movement, growth or a lasting change of heart until we have distilled and discerned our full-blooded desires and longings' (see page 68). Make a list of what you would like to think of as your true desires. Then make another list of desires which are more difficult to admit. Have any of these become idols for you? What price are you paying for this? What do these idols point you towards?

2. 'When people spurn their sexuality and its accompanying desires, they cut themselves off from that vitalizing and creative power which is fired by human sexuality (both biological and psychological)' (see page 75). We will consider this on a sociological level in the group, but you may like to think about how your sexuality is expressed and controlled in your own life. How well do you know yourself and your weaknesses in this area?

3. 'Sometimes we ... find ... that what looked so promising in prospect has crumbled and gone sour when acquired' (see page 83). Think of people to whom this has happened: how has it marked them? Have you had this experience? Looking at your time line may help focus your thoughts.

4. We have read of Augustine's breakdown. Have you ever come to the end of your tether in a particular situation? Mark it on your time line. Is there any sense of breakthrough following this experience yet?

5. What form of materialism is a temptation for you? Money in the bank? A beautiful home? Freedom to travel? Is there a token action you can take to show yourself that you are in control of your financial desires?

6. 'Desire and detachment need to interact and complement one another as the driving force and the motivating power

for long journeys of faith' (see page 80). Question 1 looked at your desires, Question 5 at your ability for detachment. Do you feel that desire and detachment complement each other in your life?

For group discussion

1. Read the story of the disciples on the road to Emmaus in Luke 24:13–35. Look at the expressions of hope, despair and then hope again.
2. Work through the questions for personal reflection, inviting comments and contributions.
3. Read again the quote at the beginning of Question 2 above. What are the positive expressions of this creative sexuality in society today? Name some of the negative expressions. What controls whether they are negative or positive? Share case histories of people (anonymously if necessary) which illustrate the positives and the negatives.

Bible passage for meditation

Look at your time line, especially at any reminders of times of breakdown or disillusionment. Then offer these experiences to God as you allow the following verses to sink into your heart.

Isaiah 61:1–3

The Spirit of the Lord God is upon me,
because the Lord has anointed me;
he has sent me to bring good news to the oppressed,
to bind up the brokenhearted,
to proclaim liberty to the captives,

and release to the prisoners;
to proclaim the year of the LORD's favour. . .
to comfort all who mourn;
to provide for those who mourn in Zion –
to give them a garland instead of ashes,
the oil of gladness instead of mourning,
the mantle of praise instead of a faint spirit.
They will be called oaks of righteousness,
the planting of the LORD, to display his glory.

THREE

Amazing Grace

> Your word is a lamp to my feet and
> a light to my path.
>
> *Psalm 119:105*

STEPPING BACK

Frequently in life, after some moving and profound experience for good or ill, we need to step back and take stock. It is rather like being on a long car journey, when there is a need from time to time to pull off the motorway for a refreshment break and to check our route on the map. On the spiritual journey we sometimes come across an important new insight, which brings with it a whole new outlook and new perspectives. It demands that we step aside to review the situation. Everything is now up for question and we need to take a fresh look at all the presuppositions on which we have built our lives to date. This, as we all discover sooner or later, is not a one-off exercise: if we are to continue travelling and making progress, then stepping back from time to time will also be part of the adventure.

The absorption of new realities and new perceptions is not always comforting or comfortable, however. It is frequently very disturbing. While we may claim to desire enlightenment and a clearer view of our inner intentions and motivations, when it actually comes to it most of us, most of the time, find the shadows more friendly and less searching than the bright light of day. Illumination shows up the cracks, and we often choose to be blind to uncomfortable facts that have been staring us in the face for years (all too obvious to our friends, of course). It can take years for us to come to that point in the road where, like Blind Bartimaeus, we are genuinely able to say, 'Let me see' (Mark 10:51). So often, like St Augustine's famous prayer for chastity, we offer a half-hearted request as a passing whim. Augustine says to God, 'I had even sought chastity from you ... and had said, "Give me chastity and continence, but not yet." For I feared that you would hear me quickly, and that quickly you would heal me of that disease of lust, which I wished to have satisfied rather than extinguished.'[1] All those resolutions to take up a healthy diet are nearly always dated 'as from tomorrow'. Or we put off that extra work we know we need to do, at least for another day. We are born procrastinators, despite Cardinal Newman's notion that 'holiness is always easier now'. We do not want to see ourselves clearly. T.S. Eliot was right to say that 'human kind cannot bear very much reality'.[2] 'This is the judgement,' says Jesus, 'that the light has come into the world, and people loved darkness rather than light...' (John 3:19). Gilbert and Sullivan put it rather more humorously: 'She may very well pass for forty-three / In the dusk with a light behind her!'[3]

We may be reluctant to see more clearly, but sometimes insight comes when we are least expecting it, and we are forced to take note, then and there. In the Bible we find such turning points in the lives of many heroes of faith. The stories of Abraham, Isaac, Jacob, Moses and Isaiah all contain dramatic moments of insight and re-evaluation. Moreover, they are never just one-off, isolated incidents: they constitute a continuous ingredient in the recipe of an enriched life. The Bible is not simply a book about what happened to particular individuals, once upon a time, a long time ago. It is a record of what is happening to most people all the time, today, tomorrow and until the end of time.

These unexpected moments of revelation break into our lives, demanding the reordering of our priorities and even, sometimes, a complete change of life. The Bible records such turning points as moments of conversion: the scales drop from our eyes and we begin to see what life is really all about. 'O God, now I see!' What we see, however, is not a different world, but the same old world from a different point of view. We see for the first time what has been there all along. The penny drops, constituting what one theologian used to call 'a cosmic disclosure'. Frequently at such moments we catch our breath; that instinctive word 'God' is suddenly on our lips – inspiration and adoration fusing into an unforgettable moment of truth, beauty or love. Perhaps we see what we have never been able to see or face up to before, or perhaps we suddenly see someone or something we have been longing to see all our life. It is at such moments that the prayer to the Holy Spirit can come to our aid: 'Enable with perpetual light, the dullness of our blinded sight.' Or, in more prosaic tones, Wesley's prayer: 'Teach me, as best my soul can bear.' In truth, we simply could not bear it, if it were to happen all at once. Hence the need for frequent times of stepping back to review our situation in the light of new information and revelation. Step by step, mile by mile, we move along the road.

Augustine took the chance to step back after the shattering episode in the garden on that summer's day in AD 386. Verecundus's villa offered Augustine just what he needed at that particular point in his spiritual journey – time and space to reflect, to step back, to retreat. It was a necessary staging post on Augustine's inner journey, before he embarked on the next stage of that journey homewards (both spiritually and geographically). Incidentally, it is perhaps not an idle reflection to note that the villa was a gift offered by a friend: in other words, it was a grace, almost a 'grace and favour' residence, where Augustine was able to ponder on God's grace towards him.

Augustine was beginning to look at the new life which is characterized far more by what God does for us, what he offers us and gives to us, than by what we do in offering ourselves back to him. Change is always the work of God's grace in our lives, freely offered, for by grace and grace alone are we saved, healed and changed 'from one degree of glory to another' in this long journey from head to heart and from heart to will. So John Newton taught us all to sing those well-known words, born of his own experience of change and conversion to the new life:

> Amazing grace! How sweet the sound
> That saved a wretch like me!
> I once was lost, but now am found,
> Was blind, but now I see.

SECOND THOUGHTS AND A CHANGE OF HEART

However much one might be tempted to rationalize the kind of inexplicable event that happened to Augustine in the garden, or indeed the sudden arrival of any new insight, it is necessarily disturbing. Many of our preconceptions go out of the window, and for a moment we lose our bearings. We speak of our world being shattered, turned upside down or back to front. At such moments there is a clear need for space to take stock and reassess our priorities. Theology and the Bible have a special word for this: that much misunderstood and misrepresented word 'repentance'. The word in Greek – *metanoia* – literally means to have second thoughts, to stop and take stock, or, as the wicked Fagan sings in the musical *Oliver!* 'I'm reviewing the situation . . . I think I'll stop and think it out again'. That is what it means to repent. It is a healthy response to a shattering new insight that necessarily results in a radical change of outlook: if our world is turned on its head, of course we will see everything from a different perspective!

That is precisely what happened to Isaiah when he went into the Temple 'in the year that King Uzziah died' (Isaiah 6:1). As a courtier, his world had fallen apart with the death of his master the king. In the course of his career, Isaiah had fallen prey to idolatry in his relationship with King Uzziah. He had allowed an earthly king and an earthly kingdom to claim his total allegiance, over and above his allegiance to the real King and to God's kingdom. (Perhaps there are echoes here of Cardinal Wolsey's sentiments in Shakespeare's *Henry VIII*: when Wolsey falls from grace, and feels his 'heart new opened', he cries out, 'Had I but served my God with half the zeal I served my King. . .'[4]) In the Temple that day, Isaiah caught a glimpse of the real King: 'Woe is me! I am lost, for I am a man of unclean lips, and I live among a people of unclean lips; yet my eyes have seen the King, the LORD of hosts!' (Isaiah 6:5) At that moment Isaiah repents – he has second and third thoughts, and probably many more. These thoughts challenge his presuppositions, his principles and his priorities, demanding that he should radically rethink what he will do with the rest of his life, in the service not of some earthly king, but of the heavenly King, the Lord of hosts. Isaiah responds to God's invitation to service knowing that his life must change: 'Here am I; send me!' (Isaiah 6:8) His whole life was turned round in response to a vision, a new insight.

That is the kind of repentance demanded by the core preaching and teaching both of John the Baptist and Jesus. Jesus summarized his mission statement with this succinct soundbite: 'The time is fulfilled, and the kingdom of God has come near; repent, and believe in the good news' (Mark 1:15). Something has happened, or something is happening, and nothing will ever be quite the same again. A response is necessary, like it or not. John the Baptist and then Jesus heralded a new order of things which demanded a radical change of lifestyle. Such life-changing events occur from time to time throughout the history of our world, and not only in individual lives. The terrorist attacks in America on 11 September 2001, for example, led *The Times* newspaper to carry out a survey on people's responses to that shattering event. In a fascinating article entitled 'Has your world really changed?' the results of the poll were revealed. One in three people living in Britain claimed that their lives had been changed 'for ever' by the terrorist attacks and that it had resulted in a 'shift in mood that makes us value our lives'. 'It has not stopped me flying,' one person was reported as saying, 'but it has made me stop and think about what I really want to do with the years I've got left.'

'It has made me stop and think about what I really want to do with the years I've got left.' You could scarcely find a better summary of what Augustine must have been saying to himself after his shattering experience in the garden, as he went 'into retreat' at his friend's villa and tried to recover the bigger picture. He needed time to rethink, time to have second thoughts on the issues and principles on which he had based his life up until then.

From September AD 386 until February 387, Augustine stayed in that country villa for a time of retreat, reflection and writing. Cassiciacum is usually identified today as Cassago Brianza, just south of Lake Como, with the Alpine peaks on the far horizon, set amidst chestnut trees, deep green wood-lands and the 'fragrance of mint and aniseed'. Frequently in later life Augustine was to recall this blessed time when he had space to draw breath, describing in detail the beauty of the autumn leaves with their deep colours of gold and saffron, and the stream choked with the dying foliage of the long summer days. It must have been quite a merry household during those months. Augustine and his friend Alypius were there, together with Augustine's son Adeodatus, then about fifteen years old. Augustine's elder brother Navigius joined them, and his cousins Rusticus and Lastidianus and two of his students, Trygetius and Licentius, both just sixteen. Needless to say, the household was presided over by the ever-watchful mother Monica!

We know a great deal about what they discussed during that time – which turned out to be a cross between a retreat and a reading party – because one of the four books that Augustine wrote that winter, *Contra Academicos,* gives us a blow-by-blow account of many of their philosophical discussions. Augustine's writings mark the progress in his thinking during those formative months. Throughout his life, he used his writing to develop his thoughts at the same time as his thoughts (i.e. his second thoughts) informed his writing. As he said in one of his letters later in life: 'I endeavour to be one of those who write by progressing and who progress by writing.'[5] *Contra Academicos* was completed in November 386, and in it Augustine tells us how his new-found faith had led him to reject the scepticism and agnosticism of the academics and to see how faith could not be achieved purely by reason but needed to go beyond reason and the activity of the intellect. He was taking another step forward on the long journey from head to heart, by allowing the flame which enlightened his mind to spread warmly into his heart.

A second book, also written during this time of retreat, was occasioned by Augustine's birthday, 13 November. 'It was consummated,' he tells us, 'during a three-day conversation,' largely in the bathhouse where, it seems, many of their discussions took place. *De Beata Vita* ('Concerning Happiness') shows that already at this stage of his pilgrimage, Augustine was quite adamant that happiness could be found only in the knowledge of God, by which he meant so very much more than mere intellectual knowledge. Now the knowledge he sought was not so much information about God, but rather the kind of knowledge that can only come through a personal relationship with God, centred on the prayer of the heart.

He wrote these two books and the scrap of another in the setting of endless discussions and reflections at Cassiciacum. As Augustine himself testifies, 'Really great things, when discussed by little men, can usually make such men grow big!'[6] He was coming to see that philosophy and metaphysics are not exclusively the property of the professionals in universities. Such matters go right to the hearts of all men and women, provided that they are willing to seek the truth, in the greater environment of the worship of the Church and through persistent prayer. Theological reflection is at its best when it is not confined to libraries and lecture rooms. It truly comes into its own when it informs and is informed by contemplative prayer and worship in the laboratory of the Church liturgy.

You cannot learn about Christianity in the same way as you can learn about history or science. Christianity is not so much something to swallow as Someone to follow. Discipleship engages every aspect of a person's being, and therefore the learning that accompanies authentic discipleship must always be done in the context of life as a practising Christian. When Luke wanted to give a description of the newly born Church at the beginning of the Acts of the Apostles, he summarized it in this way: 'They devoted themselves to the apostles' teaching and fellowship, to the breaking of bread and the prayers' (Acts 2:42). All four ingredients – and not least the fellowship – were found to be necessary if the apostolic teaching was going to take root and grow. The fellowship and worship of the Church constitute the environment in which the seeds of faith can grow and in which men and women can earnestly seek the truth, whether or not they belong to the intelligentsia.

Augustine would always contend that the Church ought not to be a galaxy of intellectuals, but rather a community seeking to live the life of truth. He would also contend that it is more likely to apprehend that truth in discussions and fellowship than in solitary, abstract speculation. There is always a need to contextualize the teaching of the Christian faith: its doctrine and creeds were not conceived by theologians pouring over books, but emerged from a praying and worshipping community. In other words, Christians experienced the faith before they formulated it. In the Orthodox churches of the East, the 'theologian' is defined as the person who prays. Make no mistake about it: theology apart from a living, corporate spirituality is dead in the water! Archbishop Anthony Bloom puts it like this: 'Theology is not knowing about God; even less is it knowing what other people have written about God. Theology is knowing God.' How can we come to know God? Only through prayer, worship and adoration.

This fuller understanding of the nature of discipleship has proved marvellously fruitful in the renewal of the churches in our own day. Popular initiatives like the Alpha Course or the Emmaus Course work so well precisely because they take place in the context of fellowship, hospitality, worship and retreat. In this way the whole person is fed and challenged by the truth – head and heart together.

'Knowledge alone cannot save us.' When St. Augustine coined that phrase nearly seventeen hundred years ago, he meant it as a principle of truth, but he was also writing a commentary on his life. Augustine as we know had two conversions, one in his head and the other in his heart. After years of experimenting with various pagan philosophies and ways of living, he was now convinced in his head that Christianity was correct. The rest of him however, was not as willing a convert. For nine more years, until he was thirty-four years old, he was unable to bring his moral life into harmony with his intellectual life faith. It is not enough just to know the truth, to have clarity of conviction, and to know where ideally our lives should be heading, though that can be a valuable start. There is also the question of heart, of energy, of willpower, of sustaining ourselves on the road.[7]

As the winter days drew on, Augustine wrote yet another book, *Soliloquies*. He describes it as his 'first intimate self-portrait', and it consists of an extended argument between his reason and his soul, or his inner self, his heart and his intuitions. Augustine's reflections in the *Soliloquies* suggest the influence of the longer nights and shorter days of winter, a withdrawal from outside pursuits and a movement towards the inner light and warmth of hearth and heart. For Augustine the momentous year, with its calendar of disillusionment and breakdown, was drawing to a close. The season seemed to reflect the inner death of the old Augustine – a death that would prefigure a new life and new beginnings, just as surely as winter prefigured spring. There was only one place to establish that new life, as Augustine knew only too well: in the waters of baptism, and at the hands of Bishop Ambrose back in Milan. It was there that all things would be made new.

In fact, he had written to Ambrose when he terminated his contract in Milan, asking the good bishop to advise him on which books of Scripture it would be best for him to study, so that he 'might be better prepared and more fitted to receive' the sacrament of baptism.[8] Ambrose had recommended the prophet Isaiah, but Augustine found the opening chapter difficult to understand and so he laid it aside for the time being. Perhaps it was a pity that he did not go on to read chapter 6, where he might have recognized something of his own journey in the record of Isaiah's vision and repentance in the Temple in that other special year, 'the year that King Uzziah died'.

In any event, the time of retreat was drawing to a close. In the spring of AD 387, it was time for Augustine to enrol in Ambrose's school, in preparation for Lent and Easter. In the fourth and fifth centuries, Lent was a season when the whole Church went back to school to prepare for the celebration of the death and resurrection of Jesus during Holy Week and Easter. People like Augustine who had not been baptized would join the Bishop's school alongside all the baptized and confirmed Christians, who would use the season of Lent to progress in their Christian discipleship. Then at Easter – early on Easter morning – the new Christians would be baptized as the sun rose, and the whole body of Christians would reaffirm their baptismal vows. Thus the making of new Christians and the renewal of old Christians went alongside each other, culminating in the glorious celebration of Easter Day.

A SCHOOL OF FAITH – EXPLORATION AND CONTEMPLATION

Being a Christian means so very much more than swallowing a few facts about Christianity and a cocktail made up of the Creed, the teaching of Scripture and Church doctrine. A believing Christian is somebody who has made the connection between the perceived world and the revealed world, between the truths and insights of everyday life and the propositions of the Christian faith, all focused in the person of Jesus Christ, the Way, the Truth and the Life.

Shakespeare, in *King Lear,* speaks of us being 'God's spies':

> [We'll] take upon 's the mystery of things
> As if we were God's spies.[9]

Such perception demands that we no longer take the world of everyday life at face value. We allow the immediate facts to point us to the ultimate reality. For the mature Christian, Christ is not external to the world of reality, waiting to be inserted into the agenda of our daily life. Rather, as well as being above and beyond all things, he is also in all things, giving to the whole of life a new significance and a richer quality. It is as though the truths of the Christian faith resonate with an earlier knowledge, in a kind of *déjà vu* experience. If Christianity is true, then it is true because it is true and not because it is Christianity. A school of faith, therefore, will not simply disseminate facts about Christianity, but will seek to make the connection between the Person of Christ and the experience of truth as already apprehended by the individual catechumen. Christianity is not an ideology; it is not a religion in the strict sense of the word, nor is it a philosophy. Christianity is not anything: Christianity is somebody. It is Jesus and the resurrection.

While there is much for the catechumen, or the new Christian, to learn about Christianity, the process will never be completed in this world. Furthermore, knowledge about Christianity does not make a Christian. Knowing Christ in a living relationship makes a Christian. The great theologian Bernard Lonergan insisted that all genuine conversion must at least involve an intellectual conversion. He was right, but it cannot stop there. Augustine had done quite a bit of intellectual homework in the course of his restless life. Now he needed to learn truth in a fuller sense, through nothing less than an encounter with the Person who is the Truth, the Way to that Truth, and Life. He needed to take on a whole new way of life.

So it was that throughout Lent in AD 387 Augustine attended the Bishop's school in Milan to learn about Christ. There he would have met others preparing for baptism, as well as a large number of Christians seeking renewal in their faith, and those who had lapsed from faith and were seeking to return to the ways of righteousness and holiness. It is good practice for all of us as Christians to go back to school from time to time, to undertake a kind of 'refresher course'. And what better time to do that than during the season of Lent, in the company of those preparing for baptism at the Easter celebrations of the death and resurrection of Jesus?

Back to Scripture, back to the Creed, back to teaching on prayer and the spiritual life, back to basics: this was what Augustine did in Milan, where Bishop Ambrose sat in his teacher's chair in the cathedral every day. In the Early Church bishops were responsible for making new Christians, as well as for making Christians new. Hence the bishop gave what we would call 'confirmation classes', acting as the 'prime minister' of God's word and sacraments, preparing the new Christians for the full rite of initiation (baptism, confirmation and first Communion) which he would administer on Easter morning.

In the course of those classes in Bishop Ambrose's school, all the teaching would point to and make a connection with the death and resurrection of Jesus Christ. That is the core belief of Christianity: that in order to enter fullness of life (or eternal life) we need to enter into the mystery of death and resurrection as exemplified in the once-for-all death and resurrection of Jesus, prefigured in his baptism in the River Jordan.

New Christians have to take hold of a totally different way of looking at life. Slowly we begin to see that real life is paradoxically all about dying and being reborn to a new quality of life. So Christ taught – much to the astonishment and bewilderment of the Jewish theologian Nicodemus, who 'came to Jesus by night' (John 3:2) – that in order to become fully human beings, we need to undergo at least two births and two deaths. The nearest analogy to this process is the transition of a caterpillar into a butterfly. The earthbound caterpillar, in some sense, dies as it becomes a chrysalis, only to be reborn in a second death/birth as an airborne butterfly.

Jesus tells Nicodemus that unless a man is born again, he cannot even begin to see the kingdom of God, let alone enter it. Elsewhere he uses another analogy: 'Unless a grain of wheat falls into the earth and dies, it remains just a single grain; but if it dies, it bears much fruit' (John 12:24). It is in the sacramental activity of baptism that a kind of second birth and premature death are assimilated. The new Christian is plunged into the waters of baptism ('buried' or 'drowned', in a sense) and raised up to new life – eternal life, abundant life of the quality promised by Christ. Rather like the caterpillar and the chrysalis, however, the new person is still encased in the old body with its limited dimensions, until that body is shed in a second death (physical death), when the new person will at last step onto the new way with an appropriate body to express fully the new quality of life beyond death. The great difficulty in all this comes from the phrase 'eternal life', which seems to suggest that the abundant life promised by Jesus begins only on the other side of the grave. That is not so. We begin that new, abundant life on the other side of the death and rebirth which we encounter in baptism, even though we do not have the new body with which to express the new life in all its fullness. Put crudely, eternal life is not so much 'pie in the sky when you die', but rather 'steak on your plate as you wait'.

As Lent progressed, therefore, Augustine, Alypius and Adeodatus could be seen daily at their classes in the cathedral, being prepared for the great day of their initiation into the life of Christian discipleship. Christian initiation in those days was a kind of package deal. As a young boy, the son of a Christian mother, Augustine would have been 'salted' – that is, a piece of salt was placed on the tongue of the newborn baby – but in North Africa at that time nearly all baptisms were of adults, usually taking place only at Easter.

There are real dangers in administering baptism exclusively to adults. In the first place, it can give the impression that we should not be baptized until we 'understand' Christianity, whatever that might mean. Of course, we shall never understand Christianity and we shall never comprehend the infinite reality of God with our finite minds. If we were to wait for such understanding, we would never be baptized. In the second place, grace is God's free, unearned gift, which we make our own by faith. Baptism is not so much a matter of comprehending faith as of being apprehended by grace and appropriating that grace by putting our faith in the Giver of the gift. As we saw earlier, the initiative is always God's, with discipleship as the response in faith and of faith. It is a paradox, but it is only in the paradox of grace that we come to a proper understanding of the Christian life. Augustine summarized the paradox with these words:

> Without God we cannot:
> Without us, he will not.

The first lesson we have to learn as would-be Christians is that we can do no good thing without God. Unless God takes a firm grip of us in the course of life's journey, there is no way that we could ever find our way to God through intellectual speculation, moral behaviour or spiritual strivings. We need to have recourse again and again to the kind of assurances expressed by Isaiah: 'For I, the LORD your God, hold your right hand; it is I who say to you, "Do not fear, I will help you"' (Isaiah 41:13).

The second lesson we must learn is that, as soon as we have apprehended that truth for ourselves, the other half of Augustine's paradox comes into play: without us, God will not accomplish his purposes for us, for the Church or for the world. 'He who created you,' wrote Augustine, 'will not save you without your co-operation.'[10] God chooses to complete his purposes only with our co-operation. He could complete his plan for the creation and redemption of the world by himself, but he has chosen not to do it without our freely willing co-operation.

When we spell this out in terms of its application to baptism, we begin to see that the apparent contradiction of baptizing both babies and adults is the best way of demonstrating this paradox of grace. As a matter of fact, in the New Testament we find that even in those very early days all ages were baptized. The jailer in Acts 16, for example, was baptized together with all his family or household, which would have included young children and slaves. It is important that this double practice of baptism is exemplified in the Church. To baptize only infants risks reducing the sacrament to the level of magic, while to restrict baptism exclusively to adults who have completed the required course reduces Christianity to the ancient heresy of Pelagianism, which tried to turn faith into a work of our own doing and the Christian life into something we have achieved for ourselves – when the Bible teaches us that faith is an entirely free, undeserved gift from God.

THE END OF THE OLD AND THE START OF THE NEW

It is, of course, very much more dramatic when adults profess their newly found faith for themselves in baptism, especially when the sacrament is administered, as it was for Augustine, after the long teachings of Lent, culminating in the Easter vigil, a dawn baptism, confirmation and first Communion in the liturgy of Easter Day.

Throughout the night, in a service which lasted from dusk to the dawn of Easter Day, the long story of God's redeeming work would have been outlined in Scripture readings, starting with Genesis and following the biblical record through the story of the exodus of God's people out of the bondage of Egypt, through the desert and into the Promised Land. These readings would have been punctuated from time to time with psalms, hymns, spiritual songs and prayers. Then, just before sunrise, the whole people of God, together with their bishop, processed from the main basilica to the baptistry singing the psalm which begins, 'As a deer longs for flowing streams, so my soul longs for you, O God' (Psalm 42:1). How very true those words are for any people who, like Augustine, have spent many years of their lives searching and straining to find the refreshing grace of God. As the procession made its way into the tomb-like baptistry of the cathedral, Augustine was at last coming home. The restless heart had found its only true and lasting peace.

The baptistry in Milan has recently been excavated in the undercroft of the present cathedral. Not unlike the private baths in the houses of the very rich, it was octagonal in shape. In the centre were three rows of steps leading down to a pool. The steps at the bottom were beautifully and colourfully decorated with fine mosaics depicting, among other things, little fish. An earlier Christian teacher from North Africa, Tertullian, had spoken most eloquently of the new Christians in those waters of the baptistry as being like little fish who, together with their great fish (*Ichthys* in Greek) Jesus Christ, 'were born again in water'. Around the edge of the baptistry ran a corridor, blazing with lamps, where each of the candidates would strip, sit in the niches of the wall and await the climax of the night's vigil – their baptism into the death and resurrection of Jesus Christ.

The bishop, for whom there was a special seat in the wall next to the pool, presided as Augustine, Alypius and Adeodatus in turn went down into the 'tomb' of baptism, to be delivered and raised from the 'womb' of the waters of regeneration, born again into new life as Christians. The waters for the ceremony of baptism had to flow freely in those days, because stagnant water (especially in hot countries) could only be the bearer of corrupted life and disease. So here indeed was a river, and the prayers and preparations for this holy night had led these new Christians (and all the old ones, too, seeking renewal and refreshment) to the point of crossing that river – their Red Sea, through which they were led from the bondage of sin through the desert to the land of promise.

'Do you turn to Christ, Augustine?' Bishop Ambrose asked as Augustine, waist deep in the water, faced the darkness of the west. 'I turn to Christ,' Augustine replied, turning from the darkness to the light, turning to the east to face the rising sun of Easter morning. 'I believe,' wrote C.S. Lewis, 'that Jesus Christ rose from the dead in the same way that I believe the sun rose this morning: not only because I can see it, but also because now I see everything else in the light of it.'

From then onwards, none of those newly baptized Christians would have been under any illusions about their status. All of them were now Red Sea Christians – men and women who had in various ways 'been through it', delivered at last from bondage as they went back into the church to be fed (with sustenance for the spiritual journey) before they set out on their pilgrimage towards the land of promise. The imagery at every point was very powerful, almost overwhelming. Fire and water, birth and death, old and new, womb and tomb – paradoxes creating a profound impact on mind, imagination and heart. Now, in the fire of faith, they could start to melt and refashion the steel of their will, twisted out of shape by sin. Actions spoke louder than words on that Easter morning: all the rhetoric, the arguments, the words of faith trailed behind the sacramental actions of the liturgy as Bishop Ambrose, like a latter-day Moses, led his new Christians back to the basilica for the climax of the Eucharist, the first Eucharist of Easter Day.

THE NEW LIFE

For the next week, as was the practice, Augustine, Adeodatus and Alypius, dressed in their white robes of chrism, attended the basilica every day to make their Communion and to hear Ambrose round off his Lent and Easter school. The exciting and demanding new life had begun. Writing of the experience many years later, Augustine said,

> We were baptized, and all anxiety over the past melted away from us. The days were all too short, for I was lost in wonder and joy, meditating upon your far-reaching providence for the salvation of the human race. The tears flowed from me when I heard your hymns and canticles, for the sweet singing of your church moved me deeply. The music surged in my ears, truth seeped into my heart, and my feelings of devotion overflowed, so that the tears streamed down. But they were tears of gladness.[11]

Clearly Augustine had been impacted by the Holy Spirit not just spiritually but also psychosomatically. Whenever we receive a fresh outpouring of God's Holy Spirit at the turning points in our Christian discipleship – and especially at baptism – it is not at all uncommon to experience some kind of physical expression of the impact of the Spirit. In the Old Testament, Sarah had a fit of the giggles, and Hannah appeared to be drunk. In the New Testament, at Pentecost, some people were given the gift of tongues as they were released in the Spirit. Tertullian speaks of the 'baptism of tears', which is clearly what Augustine experienced. Such tears are distinguishable from ordinary tears because they are essentially tears of joy not distress.

On the long journey from head to heart and from heart to will, everyone will experience roadblocks or inhibitions. No doubt, for Augustine, the tyranny of the intellect would have kept the brake on his experiences of faith, so that for him the release of the Holy Spirit would have been something beautiful and liberating. His faith would have moved from being merely intellectual to being far deeper and more overwhelming. Augustine would have realized that he was no longer in the driving seat of his own life. He was no longer in control – he who had always been in control of the direction of his life, except when his own unruly passions had taken over. Now, however, something – or rather Someone – even more powerful than his passions had taken control. There was a new sense of what the spiritual writer de Caussade called 'self-abandonment to the Divine Providence'. All this was the work of God the Holy Spirit, empowering the new Christian Augustine and equipping him for the long journey ahead. Becoming a baptized Christian is not unlike learning to swim, in so far as we shall never become real swimmers until we take our feet off the bottom and learn to live out of our depth. There is no such thing as a 'theoretical swimmer', and there is no such thing as a 'theoretical Christian'. You can be a bad swimmer and a bad Christian, but the secret in both cases is to learn to have confidence when you are out of your depth and no longer in control. That inner confidence only comes when you have finally proved for yourself that 'underneath are the everlasting arms' of God's love and grace (see Deuteronomy 33:27 NIV).

Baptism had marked for Augustine the end of the beginning. In the waters of baptism he had been brought through the Red Sea and was now about to set out through the desert towards the land of promise, led like the children of Israel by the cloud of the Holy Spirit and the bright fire of Christ, fed with the manna of the sacraments. He was heading for the promise of heaven, the ultimate destination of all Christian pilgrims – but he had not arrived. He had been made a new man and a new creation, but there was a long journey ahead. The caterpillar is not immediately changed into a butterfly – the old self overlaps with the new self for a time in a kind of no-man's-land, a between-time where, as Charles Williams put it, the 'new man' is still to some extent in 'the old way'.

The New Testament speaks of this between-time as 'post-baptismal sin', something of a theological embarrassment for those who think that the change from the old to the new is a one-stop shop. Baptized into Christ, by grace, appropriated through faith, we are indeed justified and reckoned before God as sinless, but with a righteousness not of our own. The Christian pilgrim must now press on to be sanctified by that same grace, to grow and be changed from one degree of glory to another. It is a lengthy process and frequently there are real setbacks along the way. As it said in the old Prayer Book, however, whenever we 'fall into sin' we need to 'repent and return to the Lord'. Part of our returning to the Lord is to recall and reaffirm our baptismal vows and our status in Christ. There is no need to renew the vows in the way that you would renew, say, a dog licence, because the validity of baptism never runs out – but new strength for the journey can be gained from reaffirming that we 'turn to Christ'. Our baptism is a once-for-all turning point in our Christian pilgrimage, releasing us, if we will let it, from the bondage of sin and giving us a new freedom to explore the height, length and depth of God's love and of life in all its fullness – a life of grace and holiness, which we can experience even while we pick our way along the winding road towards the land of promise.

QUESTIONS FOR FURTHER REFLECTION

Prayer of St Augustine

Oh God, from whom to be turned is to fall;
To whom to be turned is to rise;
From whom to depart is to die;
To whom to return is to revive;
In whom to dwell is to live
To reach out to whom is to love
To see whom is true possession.

For personal reflection

1. 'We often choose to be blind to uncomfortable facts that have been staring us in the face for years' (see page 96). Can you think of times when you have done this? Are you playing the ostrich about something even now?
2. Look at the key experiences you have noted on your time line. Are there any partly digested experiences you need to work through? Seek a wise friend or counsellor if this question brings up emotions you cannot handle.

3. 'Unless God takes a firm grip of us ... there is no way that we could ever find our way to God through intellectual speculation, moral behaviour or spiritual strivings' (see page 110). How can you allow God to take a firm grip?

4. 'Whenever we receive a fresh outpouring of God's Holy Spirit ... it is not at all uncommon to experience some kind of physical expression of the impact of the Spirit' (see page 114). You may be very open to this, or wary, or even quite hostile. Call to mind the experiences you have had, or have heard about, which contribute to your attitude. Ask God to make you sensitive and open to the matter for the group discussion.

5. Using Augustine's concept of a 'soliloquy', choose an area of your life where what your heart is saying differs from what your head is saying. Write a conversation between the two of them discussing the matter.

For group discussion

1. Look at Isaiah 6:1–8. What have been the turning points in your life? Choose one and consider how it has had an impact on your present situation. If no turning point is obvious, compare your life now with what it was one year, or ten years, ago. What has changed, and do you feel in control of these changes?

2. Work through the questions for personal reflection.

3. Theological reflection 'comes into its own when it informs and is informed by contemplative prayer and worship in the laboratory of the Church liturgy' (see page 102). Do we tend to leave the theological reflection to others? How can we redress the balance?

4. 'Real life is paradoxically all about dying and being reborn to a new quality of life' (see page 108). List what

things need to die in a new Christian. Which are essential and which are culturally conditioned? Would someone twenty years older or younger, or with £20,000 a year difference in income, agree with you?

5. What is the practice of your church in regard to baptism? Share memories of adult baptisms, either your own or one you have attended, or the experience of being a godparent.

6. Augustine had a long time of retreat at the villa on Lake Como. Share any experiences of different kinds of retreat: preached, individual, one quiet day, or longer. You may like to get hold of a copy of *Retreats* magazine (available from Christian bookshops) to consider the variety available and plan to treat yourself some time in the future. If this is not feasible, set aside a couple of hours to work through some of the thoughts you have had in response to these questions.

Bible passage for meditation

Your thoughts about change, or about the Holy Spirit, or about God 'having a grip' on your life may inform your meditation on this passage. Enjoy the freedom you have to experience the Spirit, and bask in his love as if you were sunbathing.

2 Corinthians 3:17–18

Now the Lord is the Spirit, and where the Spirit of the Lord is, there is freedom. And all of us, with unveiled faces, seeing the glory of the Lord as though reflected in a mirror, are being transformed into the same image from one degree of glory to another; for this comes from the Lord, the Spirit.

FOUR

The Conversion of the Heart

> Were not our hearts burning within us while he was talking to us on the road, while he was opening the scriptures to us?
>
> *Luke 24:32*

DIFFICULTIES ON THE ROAD OF DISCIPLESHIP

There is a curious occasion in the New Testament, when Jesus heals a demoniac and the man asks that he might follow Jesus and stay with him. Contrary to expectations, and against his usual practice, Jesus tells him to go home and to tell his friends and family what has happened: 'Jesus sent him away, saying, "Return to your home, and declare how much God has done for you"' (Luke 8:39). It is far more difficult for us to witness to a change of life and live out our new lifestyle as disciples of Jesus back at home, where we are still remembered as our former selves, rather than travelling into territory where our former life is unknown and we can start afresh. After all, Jesus himself testified that 'no prophet is acceptable in the prophet's hometown' (Luke 4:24).

The 'new person', therefore, will always inevitably find himself or herself in a somewhat anomalous situation. Although the convert has moved on, memories of that person's former self and habits are slow to die, both from his or her own point of view and from the perspective of friends and family. Parents are always in danger of doing this with their children, being reluctant to acknowledge sometimes that those children have grown up and have changed since they left home for college, moved away, married or progressed in a career. How much more difficult it is, then, to accept and respond creatively to profound changes in people's lives when they begin to profess a new faith.

Furthermore, the change of heart when a person comes to faith in Jesus Christ may not always be obvious at first sight. Hopefully there is indeed a genuine change of heart and outlook which is often dramatic and radical, but former sins do not just evaporate overnight. The pressing question for new Christians, therefore, is how to live with the ambivalence of the new self and sustain discipleship in an ongoing and fruitful way, with a measure of integrity.

After his baptism in Milan, Augustine set out to travel back to Rome. From there he took a ship back to North Africa, to his home country, his relatives and his friends. It is never an easy journey to take, that 'journey homewards, back to habitual self'.[1] Augustine said in one of his sermons, 'In holy baptism your sins will be forgiven, but your passions will remain; against these then you will have to fight even after you are reborn.' He continues, 'The concupiscence with which we are born will never die out as long as we live; it may grow daily weaker, but it will never die out.'[2]

That long journey from the head, with its deeply held intellectual convictions, is only the start of a much longer pilgrimage to the heart, with its ambiguous agendas and emotional tides, sometimes ebbing, sometimes flowing. As George Herbert said, 'Above all, the heart must bear the longest part.'[3] This is the longest journey – from ideas to desires, from baptism to the vision of God, when we shall finally know as we are known and become the person we were created to be. The ministry and mission of the Church have been given to pilgrims by the Pioneer of all faith journeys to help sustain them on the long path, lest they faint on the way, lose heart and give up altogether. At every point on the road, however, it is primarily our desires which fuel the journey and fire the will to press on towards the goal. Christian disciples will need to travel and to live with the daily awareness of the apparent contradiction of their status, at least in the eyes of the world. Clearly we are still sinful, with the stubborn characteristics of our former selves all too evident, but at the same time we carry with us a quiet, inner self-confidence, which can lead us to a proper self-acceptance, free from guilt. In theological terms, the Christian pilgrim is a walking sign of contradiction: justified, yet sinful.

It is the birthright of every baptized Christian to know the assurance of sins forgiven. Baptized disciples know, or should know, in a deep sense that their sins are forgiven and that they have been made acceptable in Christ to God the Father. Christians have been justified (i.e. reckoned righteous and accepted by God) by grace and grace alone, a grace which they have appropriated by faith, and this enables them to make their new baptismal status their own greatest possession. A well-known scientist who was a most faithful Christian disciple was asked on the radio what had been the greatest discovery he had made in the course of his career. He replied, 'The discovery that God loves me and that he has made me his own.'

It is important that belief and baptism are seen to belong together, whether the belief expressed is that of godparents on behalf of a child, or the mature faith of an adult who has been long in preparing for baptism. In either case, the day-to-day reality is that, justified though the newly baptized Christian may be, sin continues to be at work in contradiction to our best intentions. Even St Paul says, 'I do not do what I want, but I do the very thing I hate' (Romans 7:15). This apparent contradiction threatened to tear Paul apart, and something similar has been the experience of many committed and godly Christians in every age. How can we hold together our eternal baptismal status as sons and daughters of God with the existential reality of sinfulness, human failings and foolishness?

There are at least two wrong ways of dealing with this apparent contradiction between aims and achievements. Many people choose to give up the struggle and settle for second best, telling themselves that at least they are not hypocrites, like those people who go to church! Others rewrite ethics around their lowest moral common denominator, arguing that the best way forward is to accept yourself as you are.

The more excellent way, however, is to try to hold together the apparent contradiction between belief and behaviour by repeatedly recalling our once-and-for-all expression of faith when we were baptized into Christ. That and that alone is the foundation stone for a proper confidence in our ultimate sanctification. 'All my hope on God is founded' must be our marching song. Samuel Taylor Coleridge said, 'Faith is the affirmation and the act which binds eternal truth to present fact.' The 'eternal truth' is that I have been accepted by God the Father through grace and presented to him as sinless, while the 'present fact' is that every day I am still committing sins and falling short of my best intentions.

Two factors need to be taken seriously if I am to avoid the temptation to despair and to give up the unequal struggle. The first factor is that I must learn to rely on the all-sufficiency of God's grace, to do for me what I cannot do for myself and so, as Wesley says, 'to cover all my sin'. This does not mean that I should take for granted God's infinite forgiveness expressed once and for all upon the cross. It does mean, however, that I must learn to be strong not in my own strength, but in the strength I can find by drawing close to God daily and living by grace. The second factor is that I must learn to live a life of repentance and daily renewal, remembering that those who are forgiven much love much – and that even sins repented of can draw me closer to Christ and his reconciling work on the cross. Moral rectitude in our own strength is not only unattractive, with its tendency to self-righteousness, but it can also draw us away from Christ in a kind of do-it-yourself spirituality, light years away from the life of grace and the redemption offered by Christ.

Paul had to learn the difficult lesson that God's grace was 'sufficient' for him, and it was his much despised 'thorn in the flesh' (whether the weakness was moral or physical, we do not know) that eventually drove home for him the bitter fact that he could not keep the whole moral law through his own strength. Repeatedly on the spiritual journey, disciples are tempted to give up the struggle or to be overwhelmed by continuing failure to live up to their beliefs and morals. It is at such times that we need to recall our baptismal status in Christ and reaffirm our willingness to repent and start again. In the Prayer Book of the Episcopal Church in America, in the 'Renewal of Baptismal Vows' at the Easter Vigil Service, the question is put to the whole people of God in these words: 'Will you persevere in resisting evil, and, whenever you fall into sin, repent and return to the Lord?' Surely that sums up the Highway Code for all Christian pilgrims and disciples!

Every time we go to church, we take part in a general confession of sins and hear the gospel words of reassurance and forgiveness. In some churches at such moments, the congregation is sprinkled with water to remind everybody that they have been cleansed once and for all in the waters of baptism. In the New Testament, James exhorts us to confess our sins openly to the church (see James 5:16). Augustine, Luther and Wesley read the words of reassurance in Romans so that, as John Wesley put it, he knew that 'my sins, even my sins were forgiven'. In the Book of Common Prayer, Thomas Cranmer made particular provision for those who could not establish a good conscience by means of the general confession of sins in the course of corporate worship. In the glorious language of the sixteenth century, he exhorts such people with these words:

> And because it is requisite, that no man should come to the holy Communion, but with a full trust in God's mercy, and with a quiet conscience; therefore if there be any of you, who by this means [i.e. by the means of a general confession] cannot quiet his own conscience herein, but requireth further comfort or counsel, let him come to me, or to some other discreet and learned Minister of God's Word, and open his grief; that by the ministry of God's holy Word he may receive the benefit of absolution, together with ghostly counsel and advice, to the quieting of his conscience, and avoiding of all scruple and doubtfulness.[4]

To that end, and as James commands in his epistle, Cranmer provided in the Order for the Visitation of the Sick an appropriate form of confession of sin together with absolution, to be proclaimed by the priest in the glorious gospel words of reassurance:

> Our Lord Jesus Christ, who hath left power to his Church to absolve all sinners who truly repent and believe in him, of his great mercy forgive thee thine offences: And by his

authority committed to me, I absolve thee from all thy sins,
In the Name of the Father, and of the Son, and of the Holy
Ghost. Amen.

Such a practice is not Roman Catholic, as it is so often
assumed. On the contrary, it is a thoroughly biblical practice, though a much neglected one, and has been part of
Church practice since the earliest times, for East and West,
Catholic and Reformed alike. 'Go in peace: the Lord has put
away all your sins' are words which constitute an essential
vocabulary for travellers and pilgrims, always at risk on the
hazardous highway of faith and frequently in need of first
aid along the way.

I am certain that one of the fundamental reasons why
many people do not go to church stems from this disparity
between moral belief and moral behaviour and the inability to
square it without being or appearing to be a hypocrite. Yet
the solution is not to be found in trying to keep up external
appearances, but rather in a change of heart, which in turn
will redirect the will. The Lord promises through the prophet
Ezekiel to do for us what we cannot do for ourselves, with a
kind of spiritual heart transplant through the implanting of
his holy Word: 'A new heart I will give you, and a new spirit
I will put within you; and I will remove from your body the
heart of stone and give you a heart of flesh' (Ezekiel 36:26).
When we confess our sins, we are saying with our wills that
what we have done is not what we wanted to do, and at the
same time we are reaffirming our desire and our will to do
what is right. The good news is that, as John reassures us, 'By
this we will know that we are from the truth and will reassure our hearts before him whenever our hearts condemn us;
for God is greater than our hearts, and he knows everything.
Beloved, if our hearts do not condemn us, we have boldness

before God' (1 John 3:19–21). That gospel confidence is indispensable to every disciple of Christ on the long journey of faith.

AUGUSTINE AND THE CASE FOR GRACE

Like Paul before him and Luther long after him, Augustine rested the whole of his theological case on the reality and power of sin on the one hand, and the reality and sufficiency of grace on the other. For Augustine these were the two horns of the human moral dilemma. At one level he was pessimistic about our moral condition, but at another he was totally optimistic about the potential of God's free and undeserved gift of grace to rescue the human race from its fate.

In asserting this position and defending his theological case, Augustine challenged both the optimistic assertions of Pelagius and the pessimistic claims of the Donatists. These two opposing heresies have lurked just below the surface throughout the history of the Church, and still persist in our own day. There are times and seasons when a 'liberal' view of the human condition tempts us to believe that evil is an illusion, all in the mind, that we can achieve a moral way of life simply by exercising our willpower, and that, with a little help from God, we can shake off past habits if we are sufficiently resolute. This line of thought would claim that we were originally created good by God, and although the powers of human nature have been restricted by past habits and habitual sins, this is only a superficial condition which can be overcome through education and moral 'rearmament'. The evidence of history and the record of our own bitter experience do not endorse this optimistic and humanistic diagnosis. Clearly we need to look further and to dig more deeply.

Such humanistic optimism did flourish for a while, however, especially during the late nineteenth century, a time of bland assumption that progress – including moral progress – would automatically issue from better education and from building a better social environment. It was believed that such moral flaws as existed in our humanity were the result of nurture not nature, and that humankind would come of age given the ideal social and economic environment. These beliefs were clearly evident in such humanistic novels as *The Swiss Family Robinson,* and were implicit in the writings of Thomas Hardy and Charles Dickens.

With the dawning of the twentieth century, however, the evidence of history demanded a reversal of that optimism. Humanistic confidence suffered a bitter blow when the unsinkable *Titanic* sank – a symbol of the most powerful and invincible industrial and technological achievement of its day. Then came genocide and two world wars, and the unimaginable horrors of the Holocaust. The moral optimism of the previous generation began to look distinctly unreal. William Golding's novel *Lord of the Flies* totally contradicted the earlier moral thesis of *The Swiss Family Robinson,* with Golding placing the root of humanity's moral flaws in our nature rather than our nurture. He did this in such a way as to render traditional Church teaching on the fall far more credible and far more in keeping with the facts of history.

Both from his own experience and from his reflections on the world around him, St Augustine set his face against any such overoptimistic assessment of the human problem. As the medieval prayer puts it, he believed that 'we have no power of ourselves to help ourselves'.[5] Out of all Christ's names and titles, the one that calls Jesus the Doctor and Physician of our souls was for Augustine among the most important. He saw the work of redemption as essentially a healing process, for we are ill in the very depths of our hearts. We are wounded in the most intimate part of our being. In one of his sermons he says,

If the great Doctor came down from heaven, it is because a great patient was lying across the face of the universe. That great patient was the human race. Even the baptized man or woman must remain an invalid. Like the wounded man, near to death in the ditch in the parable of the Good Samaritan, our lives have been saved by the rite of baptism, by grace appropriated through faith, but nevertheless we must be content to endure for the rest of our lives a prolonged and precarious convalescence.[6]

Augustine expands on the parable and the analogy of convalescence by describing the Church as the 'inn' for which Christ pays the price with his life. For Augustine, all our moral faculties had been irreversibly impaired by that event in the garden of Eden, to be reversed once and for all in the garden of the resurrection. In the meantime our discipleship is lived out, if you like, between those two gardens, always relying on the sufficiency of grace and grace alone. So Augustine writes to a prosperous Christian friend: 'What ought to be more attractive to us sick men, than grace, grace by which we are healed; for us lazy men, than grace, grace by which we are stirred up; for us men longing to act, than grace, by which we are helped?'[7]

From time to time we are tempted to side more with Pelagius than with Augustine. Then suddenly, either in the history of the world or in our own lives, we come up against the power of original sin and the reality of evil, which together limit our freedom to do what is right and what, with our best selves, we would like to do. Augustine truly believed that the human race lost its freedom to want to do the right thing in that original sin of Adam. Bad news, you might suspect.

Paradoxically, however, this bad news was more than balanced by Augustine's case against the Donatists. In the last persecution of Diocletian at the beginning of the fourth century, many Christians had betrayed their faith and handed over the sacred documents of the Church to the Roman Empire, traitors to the Christian cause at a time of persecution and hostility. After AD 313, when the Roman Empire finally accepted Christianity, some Christians felt that the sin of having been a traitor was so serious that the grace of baptism could not grant forgiveness. It was necessary therefore (or so the Donatists maintained) to be rebaptized. In many ways, the austere and rigorous Augustine might have been tempted to go along with this, but once again, from his own experience, he knew in his heart that if any sin was so serious that the grace of baptism could not remove it, then there was no hope for him or for the rest of the human race. For Augustine this was the good news of the gospel: that there is no sin more powerful than grace, and the more we sin the more grace abounds. So forcefully does Paul make this same argument for the sufficiency of grace, that he almost goes over the top with an argument that comes dangerously close to 'promoting' sin so that grace may abound more and more! Fortunately he draws back at just the last moment: 'Should we continue in sin in order that grace may abound? By no means!' (Romans 6:1)

From time to time in the history of the Church there have been some who have claimed that certain sins put people beyond the pale, and from time to time in our own personal journeys we can be tempted to think that we have committed such an unforgivable sin. It is at just those moments that we most need to recall and reaffirm our baptismal status in those paradoxical words 'sinful yet justified'.

So the road of Christian discipleship passes between those two gardens – the garden of the fall and the garden of resurrection and redemption – as we live with and work through the paradox of grace.

'Twas grace that taught my heart to fear,
And grace my fears relieved.
How precious did that grace appear
The hour I first believed.

THE LIFE OF GRACE AND THE HOPE OF GLORY

When Christ ascended into the heavens, he sent the Holy Spirit down to earth, so that the things of earth would resonate with the things of heaven. The human spirit would remain in communion with the Spirit of the ascended Christ. This means that the deeds and words of God's anointed people are endorsed with the authority of Christ's heavenly rule and reign. The risen Jesus tells the disciples, 'If you forgive the sins of any, they are forgiven them; if you retain the sins of any, they are retained' (John 20:23). Much earlier Jesus had said, 'Whatever you bind on earth will be bound in heaven, and whatever you loose on earth will be loosed in heaven' (Matthew 16:19). Now, as the risen Lord prepares his disciples for his heavenly departure, he reassures them that they will still be in touch with him.

If anything, from now onwards, they will be even closer to their Lord by the anointing of the Holy Spirit, because the Lord's presence will no longer be restricted to time and place as it had been during his incarnate, earthly ministry. Christ's disciples will literally be with their ascended and reigning Lord in spirit. They will experience the dynamic working of the Holy Spirit within them, through them and beyond them, 'at all times and in all places'. The Holy Spirit will make Jesus present, through Christ's Spirit-filled Body, the Church, through the Scriptures, through the sacraments, through personal prayer and corporate worship, through the loving service of others. So Jesus promises: 'I will not leave you orphaned ... But the Advocate, the Holy Spirit, whom the Father will send in my name, will teach you everything [i.e. will continue my teaching ministry to you], and remind you of all that I have said to you' (John 14:18, 26). The Holy Spirit assures us of the continuing, real presence of Jesus through the appointed means of grace, bringing with him the assurance of the hope of future glory.

What a glorious difference the Holy Spirit makes to the dynamic of our faith! Once and for all at their baptism, Christian disciples will receive him ('Receive the Holy Spirit'), yet this is also an ongoing process, as the bishop exhorts the candidates in the service of Confirmation: 'Daily increase in his Holy Spirit more and more until you come to his everlasting Kingdom.' It is the work of the Holy Spirit to overshadow us as well as to indwell us, so that, like the Blessed Virgin Mary, Christ is formed within us (see Luke 1:35). As mentioned in the previous chapter, as we daily increase in the life of the Holy Spirit of God we will very likely experience psychosomatic 'symptoms' of the release that the Spirit brings. We may feel that 'strange warming of the heart' that eventually fires the will, or we may receive the gift of laughter in the Spirit, or the gift of tears. Some people experience being 'slain in the Spirit', or give the appearance of drunkenness. Some are given the lovely gift of tongues as they pray, released from the bondage of words and the tyranny of the cerebral process into the language of love. In these and many other ways, disciples of Christ experience the intimate and real presence of Jesus through the work of the Holy Spirit.

The Holy Spirit makes the incarnate Christ contemporary in the here and now, in the bread and wine of everyday life, bringing the Risen Lord even closer to us than he was to his first disciples when he was on earth. By the Holy Spirit, earth and heaven are now one flesh, 'married' in the incarnate and ascended Christ. Yes, indeed, what a difference the Holy Spirit makes!

Without the Holy Spirit
God is far away
The gospel is a dead letter
The Church is simply an organization;
Authority a matter of domination
Mission a matter of propaganda;
The liturgy, no more than an evocation;
Christian living, a slave mentality.

But in and with the Holy Spirit
The cosmos is resurrection and groans
with the birth pangs of the Kingdom.
The risen Christ is here and now.
The gospel is the power of life;
The Church shows forth the life of the Trinity;
Authority is a liberating service;
Mission is a Pentecost.
The liturgy is both memorial and anticipation
Human action is deified.[8]

Throughout history, whenever we (either individually or the Church as a whole) have ignored the power and working of the Holy Spirit, Christianity has shown the unacceptable face of unredeemed religion at its very worst, suppressing and oppressing the human spirit. Hearts harden into formalism, and rigidity and aridity take over from a proper freedom in the Spirit. Means become ends; icons intended to point beyond themselves degenerate into idols, drawing attention to themselves and their own glory. It is so important to remember that the Church, the sacraments, the Bible, prayer, preaching and service are all means not ends, icons not idols, intended to point us towards and bring us into the real presence of the Lord, who is beyond all our images and imaginings. They are intended to point us to Jesus, for if Jesus is not Lord of all, he is not really Lord at all. He must be Lord of the

Church, Lord of the Scriptures, Lord of the sacraments and Lord of the universe.

Whenever I am trying to get my cat to look at something and I point to that object, he simply will not look at it. Instead, he stubbornly looks at my finger. There are Christians just like my cat! They look at the Scriptures rather than through them to the One to whom they point. As Jesus said to the Pharisees, 'You search the scriptures because you think that in them you have eternal life; and it is they that testify on my behalf. Yet you refuse to come to me to have life' (John 5:39–40). It cannot be said too often that Christianity is not a religion of the book. It is instead a matter of faith in the Person who has chosen to reveal himself uniquely through a book, the Scriptures. And by his mercy, God has given us his Holy Spirit with specially anointed means and pointers through which Christ is made present to us.

1. THE CHURCH

I love the Church of God; it is the mother of my faith and it is through the Church that I came to know Jesus Christ as my Saviour and Lord. But I love the Church most when it talks least about itself and most about Jesus. The Church is supremely a means of grace and not an end in itself. It is intended to point us to that kingdom that has no end, and to enable Christ's disciples, through the word and the sacraments, to live the lifestyle of the kingdom 'on earth as it is in heaven'. St Augustine wrote, 'Let us love the Lord our God, let us love his Church: he, like a father, she, like a mother; he, like a master, she, like a servant, for we are the children of this very servant.'[9] Something very dark occurs when the roles of 'master' and 'servant' are reversed, as has happened frequently in the course of history and sadly still happens today. 'Churchianity' is a terrible distortion of Christianity, yet sadly it has always had many followers.

Of course, the Church is made up of more sinners than saints – it is very much a mixed bag! It is no good looking for the perfect church: it does not exist, and even if it did, the moment you or I joined it that church would no longer be perfect. Essentially the Church on earth is made up of travellers and pilgrims, who are hopefully making progress as 'followers in the Way' but have clearly not arrived at their final destination. Saints and sinners alike have a mighty long way to go.

2. THE SCRIPTURES

The Scriptures are a wonderful gift from God, a unique means of grace, a very special icon pointing the way to Jesus. Paul writes to Timothy, 'Continue in what you have learned and firmly believed, knowing from whom you learned it, and how from childhood you have known the sacred writings that are able to instruct you for salvation through faith in Christ Jesus' (2 Timothy 3:14–15). Notice that salvation itself is through faith in Jesus, through the instruction of the Scriptures. 'All scripture is inspired [breathed into, not dictated] by God and is useful for teaching, for reproof, for correction, and for training in righteousness, so that everyone who belongs to God may be proficient, equipped for every good work' (2 Timothy 3:16–17).

We are not asked to believe in the Scriptures, but rather to believe in Jesus Christ, who makes himself uniquely revealed and present to us through the Bible. (It is almost as though we have to learn to read this book 'between the lines'.) Undoubtedly the Bible is a 'charismatic' book, a book of presence which, when read by a heart anointed with the Holy Spirit, points to Jesus and brings us into his real presence in much the same way that the sacraments point to Jesus and bring us into his presence.

Augustine had a very high doctrine of the Scriptures, following his experience in the garden outside Milan when he opened the Bible and the words sprang off the page. Through those words, Jesus – the Word made flesh – made himself present to Augustine, so much more than a mere idea or dogma. It was a never-to-be-forgotten personal encounter. The real presence of Jesus, coming through the words of Scripture, at last accomplished what all the words of the preachers and the prayers of his mother had failed to do. From his own experience, therefore, Augustine always insisted that our reading of Scripture should be brought before the bar of Christ, the Lord of Scripture: 'We should bring everything to Christ if we want to walk on the right path of intelligence ... If, in a particular passage of scripture, we can't understand the meaning, let us not separate it from Christ ... as long as we have not come to find Christ, we have not truly understood the text.'[10]

As much as Augustine loved the Scriptures, he loved the Word of God – Jesus – more. So, as Cyprian Smith says in *The Path of Life,* reading Scripture is not 'like reading tarot cards or consulting the I-Ching'. He goes on:

> In those non-Christian forms of divination all we are looking for is an answer to the problem perplexing us; the question of who it is who is speaking or providing the answer matters very little. Proper bible reading puts us in touch with God, it establishes a relationship with him, just as prayer does and also as the sacraments of the church do. It is a meeting point, a place of encounter.[11]

We therefore need to 'pray' the Scriptures, not just read them, because our reading of Scripture should always be undertaken in the presence of Christ, the Lord of Scripture. We must do as the ancient prayer of the Church bids us and regularly read Scripture, 'mark, learn and inwardly digest it', for in Scripture itself we are told to receive it into the 'ears' of our hearts and to have it grafted onto our hearts. Again and again throughout the New Testament, we are told to *receive* the word of God and not merely to hear it or listen to it. 'Welcome with meekness the implanted word that has the power to save your souls' (James 1:21).

Archbishop Cranmer, in the Book of Common Prayer, clearly wanted Christians to know off by heart at least four quotes from Scripture which embodied the good news of the gospel. He calls these four quotes 'comfortable words', when the celebrant in the Communion Service is instructed to say, 'Hear what comfortable words our Saviour Christ saith unto all that truly turn to him.' Then follow these four key New Testament texts, two from the Gospels, one from Paul and one from John.[12] All of them are intended to reassure Christian disciples of God's loving salvation and redemption, and are meant to be learned by heart. We all need such words of reassurance, and texts we know by heart are enormously helpful in times of crisis, temptation or pain. During his wilderness temptation, Christ countered the devil's words with words from Scripture three times, prefaced each time with the words, 'It is written. . .' Again, when Christ was dying on the cross, three of his last words were phrases from Scripture, learned long before and now, in his time of need, released into his conscious mind to bring him comfort.

3. SACRAMENTS

As with the Bible, it is also through, rather than in, the sacraments of the Church that we encounter the real presence of Christ. Again this is essentially the work of the Holy Spirit, who 'overshadows' (*episkiadzo* in Greek) the elements of bread and wine in the Eucharist in just the same way as the Holy Spirit overshadowed Mary at the Annunciation, and to the same end – to form Christ and the Body of Christ. In the Eastern Churches, the Coptic Church and the ancient Celtic Church, the calling down of the Holy Spirit over the elements of bread and wine constitutes a dramatic and visible action to replicate the sense of 'the wind of the Spirit' – waving hands over the bread and wine. In the Western Churches the celebrant simply extends hands over the bread and wine. The different practices are of no account, however. The important factor is what they signify: the activity of the wind of the Spirit and the overshadowing of the Holy Spirit in effectively making Jesus truly present through the eating and drinking of the bread and wine. This is the same Holy Spirit who warmed the hearts of Cleopas and his friend at Emmaus when they recognized Jesus as the Risen Lord at 'the breaking of the bread'.

For Christians, therefore, the Eucharist is an especially intimate encounter – the most intimate encounter we could ever imagine with our Risen and Ascended Lord. Yet it should always be perceived and received as essentially the work of the Holy Spirit, who lifts us with our heavenly food into the presence of the Lord. 'Man is what he eats,' said the cynical and secular philosopher Ludwig Feuerbach. Little did he realize that his statement is precisely the emphasis that Jesus gives – much to the offence of the crowd – in his eucharistic teaching throughout the sixth chapter of John's Gospel. As Augustine said, 'We eat the Body of Christ, in order to become the Body of Christ.' On another occasion he said, 'You are the Body of Christ. That is to say, you must be taken, blessed, broken and given in order that you may partake of the divine Charity.'

Thus the work of the overshadowing Holy Spirit forms, if you like, three bodies of Christ. First, there is the Body of Christ in the womb of the Virgin Mary at the Annunciation and the conception of Jesus. Second, there is the Body of Christ in the Eucharist, when the celebrant calls down the

Holy Spirit to overshadow the elements of bread and wine. Finally, and perhaps most wonderfully, there is the Church, the people of God, when the bishop stretches his hands over the heads of the confirmation candidates, overshadowing them and proclaiming in the familiar words: 'We are the Body of Christ; by the one Spirit we were all baptized into one Body.' So the three bodies – physical, sacramental and mystical – all constitute one glorified Body of the Ascended and Reigning Christ in glory, enabling Paul to declare with conviction: 'Christ in you, the hope of glory' (Colossians 1:27).

As the Israelites needed food from heaven to sustain them for their journey through the wilderness to the Promised Land, so the new Israel, the Church of God, needs food for the journey of discipleship through the 'desert' of this world, on their way to the City of God, the New Jerusalem. 'Go forth upon thy journey, Christian soul,' says the minister at the final commendation in the funeral rites in many churches.

4. THE MINISTRY OF HEALING

Healing should be seen as central to the ministry and mission of the Church as a whole, and not as some rarefied ministry for extra-special Christians only. Christ's charge to his disciples was twofold: to preach the gospel and heal the sick. The two ministries belong together. This becomes especially obvious when we dig deeply into the meaning of the word *soteria* in Greek, which is almost always translated as 'salvation'. Yet 'health' is perhaps a better translation of the root word. In his translation of the Scriptures into English, William Tyndale renders 'salvation' as 'health', 'saved' as 'healed', and 'Saviour' as 'Physician'. Thus in Luke's account of the visit by Jesus to the house of Zacchaeus (Luke 19), Tyndale translates verse 9 as, 'Today, health has come to this house'. Had we kept Tyndale's 'health' and 'healed' throughout the Bible instead of 'salvation' and 'saved', the ministry of the Church would have been seen as something very much broader than it is usually understood to be.

In the New Testament, the preaching ministry is seen in the much fuller context of ministry to the whole person. Jürgen Moltmann engagingly describes health, healing and salvation as 'an ever-varying round dance of the redeemed in the Trinitarian fullness of God, the complete harmony of soul and body'.[13] The mandate for this whole ministry is clearly stated in the Epistle of St James: 'Are any among you sick? They should call for the elders of the church and have them pray over them, anointing them with oil in the name of the Lord' (James 5:14). Here again is implied the ministry we see in the Book of Acts when the apostles lay hands on the sick in imitation of what they have seen Christ doing during his earthly ministry. Here again is the overshadowing of the Holy Spirit so that Christ may be formed in the sick person, bringing health and healing. It is heartening to notice in recent years how so many branches of the Church, across the spectrum of traditions, have recovered this ministry of healing.

5. THE PRAYER OF THE HEART

'Prayer is not thinking much,' said St Teresa of Avila. 'Prayer is loving much.' Once we get that principle right, the question of whether to use words or not becomes secondary. Prayer is essentially an expression of love – possibly the ultimate expression and certainly the most far-reaching. Where there is a lack of love, prayer is impossible. We learn to pray just as we learn to love. 'Prayer, true prayer,' writes Jaime Garcia, 'is completely oriented towards God. But to orient our desires towards God is the result of conversion. That is why we must never separate prayer from conversion.' Augustine's conversion was a conversion to the prayer of the heart, and of the most passionate desires of his heart at that – a heart which was slowly learning to love and to be loved. The most essential element of prayer is simply 'being with Jesus', not necessarily with an agenda or a shopping list of wants, likes and dislikes, but just being in the presence of the Lord. My cat has taught me a great deal about prayer. He just loves to be close to me and in my presence, though no words pass between us.

Augustine was fortunate in that he learned to pray as a boy, and even in his early days he learned that we need to pray to God not just with a few ideas off the top of our head, but rather with all our heart. So he tells us, 'As a boy, I began to pray to you, my help and my refuge, and by invoking you, I broke the knots which bound my tongue. As a little child, with an ardour that was not small, I prayed to you that I might not be beaten at school!'[14] Not exactly a prayer of the highest aspirations, you might say, but nevertheless a prayer starting in the only way it can. As Pere Grou said, you can only 'pray as you can, and not as you can't'!

Augustine never ceases inviting us to enter into the heart, for it is in the heart that Christ, the Master of the interior, speaks to us and teaches us in ways that cannot be put into words: 'Christ is inside you, his dwelling is there. Present him with your prayer, but don't act as if he is far away. The wisdom of God is never far away ... Yes, it is within the deepest part of yourself: let your prayer flow before him and he will hear.'[15]

As we grow in prayer, seeing it as developing an intimate and mature relationship with God, we begin to dwell less on what we want and much more on the One whom we want. So Augustine writes,

> God wants a disinterested following, freely-given love, that is, pure love. He does not want to be loved because he gives something outside of himself, but because he gives of himself. One who invokes God in order to become rich

does not invoke God; he invokes what he wants for himself. When you say: 'God, give me wealth,' you don't want God himself to come to you, you want the wealth to come to you. What you want to come to you is what you invoke. If, to the contrary, you invoke God, he will come to you himself and he will be your wealth. But, in reality, you want to have your treasure chest filled and your conscience empty. God doesn't fill treasure chests, but hearts.[16]

So the prayer of the heart keeps the feet of disciples moving on that long journey from head to heart and from heart to will, for it kindles and fires up our desires while also redirecting them. Our desires at first are necessarily somewhat self-centred – as is all our loving in our immaturity. Then, as we move along our journey of faith and discipleship, we befriend those early, basic desires and let the love of the Holy Spirit redirect them to God for his own sake, and through him to all those whom we are called to love on his behalf. Some are called to love the One through one, as in marriage or deep friendship; some are called to love the One through many, as in celibacy and wide friendship. Yet all alike are called to love the One, so that to stop praying is to stop loving, and to stop loving is to stop living. Augustine wrote, 'Begin to love . . . as the amount of love grows in you . . . you begin to feel God'[17] And again, 'You are the life of souls, the Life of lives. You are within me, more deeply than my deepest soul.'[18] So deep did this yearning and longing prayer go in Augustine that at one point in mid-life he exclaims,

Too late have I loved thee . . . You were within and I was outside and it was there that I was looking for you, and I threw myself, disgraced as I was, upon the grace of the things you have made. You were with me, but I was not with you; these things kept me far away from you, things which would not have existed if they had not existed in you.[19]

6. PREACHING

It was the faithful preaching of Bishop Ambrose, from his chair in the cathedral of Milan, that first touched the heart of Augustine, long before the dramatic turning point in the garden. The preacher of God's holy Word should always remember the awesome responsibility of this ministry. You never know who will hear God's Word spoken especially to them, through the inadequate words of your next sermon! As Paul said, 'Woe to me if I do not proclaim [preach] the gospel!' (1 Corinthians 9:16) Augustine said in one of his sermons, 'The Holy Gospel which we heard just now as it was being read has admonished touching the remission of sins. And on this subject, must you be admonished now by my discourse. For we are ministers of the word – not our own word, but the Word of our God and Lord.'[20]

From the outset, says Augustine, the preacher must approach his or her calling with awe and with a sense of the transcendent. Information is not enough; at some point it must give pride of place to inspiration and proclamation. So, he says,

> The sound of our words strike the ear, but the Master is within. You must not think that anyone learns from a man. The noise of our voice can be no more than a prompting; if there is no teacher within [the Holy Spirit, supremely], that noise of ours is useless ... Outward teachings are but a kind of help and prompting: the teacher of hearts has his chair [cathedra] in heaven.[21]

The salvation of the preacher is itself tied up with the salvation of the people. Preacher and people wear, if you like, the same pilgrim shoes. Here is Augustine again:

> Why do I preach? Why do I sit here upon the cathedra? What do I live for? For this one thing alone, that we may

142

one day live with Christ! This is my endeavour, my honour, my fame, this is my joy and my treasured possession! And if you have not heard me attentively, and I for all that not remained silent, then I have at least saved my own self, but I do not desire to attain everlasting salvation without you.[22]

On another occasion, with a similar burning passion, Augustine exclaimed, 'Preach wherever you can, to whom you can and as you can.'[23]

Preaching is so much more than teaching, though it will also involve teaching, of course. In an unforgettable phrase, Augustine described the sermon as an event in which 'one loving heart on fire sets another heart on fire'. Rightly understood, preaching is a unique means of grace in which the hearers are not simply an audience, but participate, interact and respond. Indeed, Augustine claimed that there were only two fitting responses to the sermon: either it should bring the congregation 'to its feet to confess their faith', or 'to their knees to confess their sins'.

A sermon is not an essay, stringing together several ideas largely addressed to the mind. It should enlighten the mind, yes, but it should also warm the heart and fire the will to repent and reorientate one's life. Therefore the language of the sermon – like the language of Christ's parables – is not abstract, but uses symbolism to fire the imagination. Augustine knew instinctively that he was in the business of planting for eternity, so he knew that his preaching must plant seeds of God's Word in the imagination and heart of the congregation. He understood the need for vivid images and allegories which could make the sermon resonate with the subconscious as well as conscious experiences of his hearers, and which would help them to make the connection between things and experiences previously unconnected. All this is a further and vital activity of what Bishop John Taylor used to call 'the Go-Between God' – the Holy Spirit.

Clearly the preaching of God's Word is a precious and awesome means of grace to strengthen, direct and motivate pilgrims and would-be disciples of Christ. Preacher and pilgrim alike neglect this precious gift at their peril.

7. OTHER SIGNPOSTS FOR THE PILGRIM

Stimulated and revitalized by these various and specific means of grace by which God sustains his disciples on their journey, the wise pilgrim who uses the Church with its word and sacraments will increasingly discover all kinds of other pointers in the world at large. 'Worship,' wrote Archbishop William Temple, 'includes all life and the moments spent in concentrated worship, whether in church or elsewhere, are the focusing points of the sustaining and directing energy of the worshipper's whole life.'[24] Jesus did not come to give us 'church life', but to enrich the whole of our lives, every day, not just one day a week. 'I came that they may have life, and have it abundantly' (John 10:10).

The enriched life, the life anointed with the Holy Spirit, will make all kinds of connections through the symbolism of music, art, poetry, sculpture, drama and literature, so that we will see, in the words of Gerard Manley Hopkins, that

> The world is charged with the grandeur of God.
> It will flame out like shining from shook foil.[25]

We might do well to remember that at the first Pentecost, through the work of the same Holy Spirit who attended creation at the outset, they all heard the wonderful deeds of God 'in their own language'. There was a time when the Church was much more explicitly a patron of the arts, but in recent years that connection has been considerably weakened. We should not despise the language of the arts to convey the wonders of God, not least to this postmodernist generation, as we pursue truth, goodness *and* beauty as signs of the work of the Holy Spirit. The Church has put many of its gospel eggs in the basket of truth and goodness, but has been in serious danger since the time of the Reformation of ignoring the witness of beauty. There is much work to be done in the coming years on this front.

God uses all kinds of resources – sometimes the most unlikely – to prompt us and push us, to motivate us and give us the necessary resources of grace and love to sustain us on our long journey of faith. Indeed, one of the biblical titles for the Holy Spirit is the 'Comforter' – a Middle English word which originally meant much more than the word 'comfort' does today. In the Bayeux Tapestry, the words along the bottom describe King Harold as 'comforting' his troops. In this context the word indicates that he was exhorting his troops to go on and do even better. That is precisely the work of the Holy Spirit – to energize, motivate and fire our will to achieve the redirected desires of our hearts.

Little wonder, therefore, that for the disciple with eyes and ears fully open to God through the empowerment of the Holy Sprit, the world is daily full of surprises. Frederick Buechner's prayer is apt: 'Lord, catch me off guard today. Surprise me with some moment of beauty or pain, so that at least for the moment I may be startled into seeing that you are here in all your splendour, always and everywhere, barely hidden, beneath, beyond, within this life I breathe.'

In the Early Church, the bishop who was preparing the candidates for baptism at Easter had a special ceremony to conduct on mid-Lent Sunday. The Gospel of the day was always the story of the opening of the deaf man's ears with the word *ephphatha* (see Mark 7:31–7). After this had been read, the bishop anointed the eyes and ears of the baptismal candidates, using the same word, *ephphatha,* and offered a prayer that the new Christians would be more open to hear and see the glory of God in his creation. This was intended to fire up all five of their senses, and most certainly not to cool down their desires. Thus we sing, 'Breathe through the heat of our desires. . .' and again, 'What is rigid gently bend; what is frozen warmly tend; straighten what goes erringly.' As we walk the way of faith, the work of the Holy Spirit and the attendant means of grace should make us increasingly open to God, and daily more sensitive to him, to others and to the whole created order.

QUESTIONS FOR FURTHER REFLECTION

Prayer of St Augustine

O Thou, who fillest heaven and earth, ever active, ever at rest, who art present everywhere and everywhere art wholly present; who art not absent even when far off, who with thy whole being fillest yet transcendest all things, who teachest the hearts of the faithful without the din of words; teach us, we pray Thee, through Jesus Christ our Lord. Amen.

For personal reflection

1. 'Former sins do not just evaporate overnight' (see page 120). Which struggles took time? Which are ongoing? Find a way of representing this on your spiritual time line.
2. 'The pressing question ... is how to live with the ambivalence of the new self and sustain discipleship in an ongoing

and fruitful way, with a measure of integrity' (see page 120). How do you maintain integrity if your faith ceases to feed you, or if you feel that your marriage is dead, or if you have outgrown your job? What does integrity mean in these cases? Where does the rubber hit the road in your life?

3. Make a personal statement of what the following mean to you in your spiritual life. Does this section in the book (see pages 130–47) include any new angles for you, or anything with which you disagree? Does what you say throw up any inconsistencies in your practice about which you feel challenged?

> The Church
> The Scriptures
> Sacraments
> The ministry of healing
> The prayer of the heart
> Preaching

4. What does the general confession mean to you in the context of the weekly service? (Or any part of your regular service which serves this function.) Do you ever feel the need for the sacrament of reconciliation administered personally by a priest, as advised in the Anglican Book of Common Prayer?

For group discussion

1. Read 2 Timothy 3:14–17. Share what the major influences on your Christian life have been. In what sense are the Scriptures 'inspired by God': dictated to men who acted as word-processors, a mythical telling of God's side of the story, or somewhere in between?

2. Work through the questions for personal reflection, sharing what you feel about the insights you have gained and the challenges you have faced.
3. Share your church tradition on confession, and if you all go to the same church, discuss any other practices you know of. Is there any matter which you would like to share with someone in this personal way? If you do not feel at home with this, consider writing a letter to God about what is troubling you.

Bible passage for meditation

This Old Testament promise speaks of a change of heart in a very real sense. Look at your time line and remember some of your key experiences of this process. Thank God for every one of them, and invite him to go on with this work, showing you any changes you need to make at this stage of your life.

Ezekiel 36:26

A new heart I will give you, and a new spirit I will put within you; and I will remove from your body the heart of stone and give you a heart of flesh. I will put my spirit within you, and make you follow my statutes and be careful to observe my ordinances.

FIVE

Vocation and Sanctification

> No one has greater love than this,
> to lay down one's life for one's
> friends.
>
> *John 15:13*

It must have seemed very strange to Augustine when he finally returned to North Africa and his hometown of Thagaste, late in AD 388. The homecoming party constituted a tight little group of Augustine and his friends, together with his son Adeodatus, but now conspicuously without the matriarchal figure of Monica, who had died before they reached home. They settled on a portion of Augustine's family estate to live the life of baptized, dedicated laymen in close association with the local Catholic church. It had always been impossible to think of Augustine *not* having his friends around him and living some kind of community life, and so it was to continue, at least for the time being.

Nebridius had returned to North Africa with the rest of the party, but he was unable to settle down in Thagaste and felt obliged to return to his country house near Carthage to take care of his ageing mother. Augustine stayed in contact with Nebridius by letter, and it is abundantly clear from their correspondence that Augustine and his little community of friends were continuing to pursue their spiritual journey, but now from a point on the road of discipleship well beyond where they had been spiritually during their endless discussions back in Cassiciacum. There the little band of participants had resembled a gathering of philosophers more than a religious community. That was no longer the case.

The correspondence between Nebridius and Augustine is extensive and fascinating. Nebridius apparently failed to realize how very much Augustine had moved on in his spiritual journey, and still clung to an understanding of Augustine's community as being essentially a gathering of free-spirited philosophers. 'It gives me the greatest pleasure to keep hold of your letters as if they were my own eyes,' he writes. 'Some shall speak to me of Christ, some of Plato, some of Plotinus.' Yet during the two years that Augustine spent at Thagaste with his little community, we can perceive a radical change of outlook. Not surprisingly, Nebridius, with his pagan background, was a little 'stuck' in endless philosophical questionings. Augustine, by contrast, was moving on from the privileged, self-serving life of philosophical speculation towards a deeper commitment to a life of service as a disciple of the One who says at every turning in the road, 'Follow me'. It is significant that the fledgling Augustinian community was to become known as the 'Servants of God'. Increasingly committed to a radical reappraisal of his life's priorities, Augustine sought in his letters – with eagerness and even impatience – to lead Nebridius forward to the path that he had discovered.[1]

In one letter Nebridius urges Augustine to live alone with God and to nurture his own spiritual growth. Augustine retorts somewhat sternly that he must stay committed to 'those whom I feel it would be quite wrong to desert'.[2] Baptism and all that went with it had moved Augustine on from the paralysis of analysis towards a life of action and service. It could be said that baptism is a kind of ordination service, when we move from an individualistic faith into a corporate expression of that faith, through worship, fellowship and the service of God and of others (see Acts 2:42). Of course there is a time to sit and reflect, a time for retreat, but there is also a time to act on our reflections, in a life dedicated to the service of God's kingdom. What now occupied Augustine's mind was the nature of that dedicated service.

Augustine was strongly tempted to withdraw into a kind of spiritual ghetto, into semi-retirement, and at first he actually urges on Nebridius the need to set his sights on growing 'godlike in . . . retirement'. After all, Augustine was now approaching forty which, in terms of the life expectancy of his day, would have been equivalent to our late fifties. Moreover, in the declining years of the Empire, many who could afford it were sorely tempted just to 'drop out' and seek the quiet life. It was not, in truth, a suitable option for the restless Augustine. He was indeed still restless, still seeking God's purposes for him. Where on earth was his spiritual journey leading him?

Peter Brown comments, 'The centre of gravity of Augustine's thought had begun to shift. He had returned to Africa without his text-books, and his schemes for an intellectual programme based on the Liberal Arts now seemed distant.'[3] Then something occurred which seemed to indicate that Augustine must pull up the tent pegs of a comfortable existence in the backwaters of Thagaste and enlist in the Lord's active service. Within only a year or so of settling down in Thagaste, death struck and Augustine lost his close friend

Nebridius and his teenage son Adeodatus. With the loss of his mother and his son, Augustine had no ties or responsibilities.

Clearly God was asking something more of Augustine, and a feeling of unsettlement once again took hold of his pilgrim spirit. To return to Chesterton's image, the pub was once more pointing back to the road. Augustine could not and must not stand still, but must take to the road and the furthering of his spiritual journey. Peter Brown writes, 'It may well be that grief and a sense of emptiness now pressed Augustine into a more active life.'[4] Augustine was clearly no longer content to pursue a purely academic and philosophical way of life. 'Let us put off all empty duties, and take on useful ones,' he wrote. 'As for exemption from care, I do not think that any can be hoped for in this world.'[5]

There is considerable evidence – medical and otherwise – to suggest that retirement in any form is potentially a spiritually hazardous time in life. Many people do indeed become ill when they retire. Perhaps a married couple might tell themselves that once they have got the children safely off their hands, and the parents-in-law tucked up in a nursing home, they can then sit back a bit and enjoy each other's company for its own sake. The fact that it seldom works out quite so happily is not totally accidental. A self-serving partnership, whether of marriage or friendship, is destined to decay unless it looks to new challenges and opportunities for altruistic service.

Perhaps it is not too much of an exaggeration to say that the difference between Christian spirituality and the 'popular' spirituality of today is to be found in precisely this point. Christian spirituality is not concerned with the feel-good factor or a 'spiritual massage', but much more with seeking opportunities for service and ministry to and for others. Jesus turns this reality into a paradox when he claims, 'Those who want to save their life will lose it, and those who lose their life for my sake will find it' (Matthew 16:25).

Whatever gifts we are given in God's loving providence, they are always given to us in order to be given away, not to be hoarded as some kind of spiritual investment policy. 'He saved others, he cannot save himself' is the paradox running through vocation and ministry in all its many forms. Very often, in practice, it is as though we are saved by saving others. For each of us, our distinctive vocation to service is the means by which God styles our ultimate sanctification. In the New Testament Jesus teaches that service is the heart of the matter from start to finish.

Peter Brown summarizes this transitional period in Augustine's spiritual pilgrimage by saying that by the end of the brief time with his little community in Thagaste (only about three years), Augustine 'was a lonely man, entering middle age, who had lost much of his past and who was groping, half-consciously, for new fields to conquer'.[6] With the benefit of hindsight, it is not difficult to see why the restless heart of Augustine would refuse to settle down in the domesticity of a quiet life – not even an enclosed community life.

LIVING FOR OTHERS

As Archbishop William Temple expressed so very succinctly, 'The Church is the one society that exists for the sake of those who are not members of it.' The Church must never fall into the trap of becoming a ghetto, set apart behind a drawbridge, fostering that fatal fortress mentality. Most other societies in the world exist to promote the interests of their own members. The very process of our evolution as the human race has encouraged the attitude of 'every man for himself' in the battle for the survival of the fittest. Here in Britain, the individualistic consumerism promoted by Margaret Thatcher and her

Conservative government in the late twentieth century strongly encouraged just this kind of rat race: look after yourself first.

Perhaps the process of 'every man for himself' was essential in the early days of evolution. Yet the claim of Christianity would be that evolution cannot come to perfection and realize its true end in reflecting the life of the Creator, unless a complementary (and contradictory) dynamic enters into the evolutionary chain – namely altruism, or unselfishness. Altruism is the only thing that can rescue evolution from self-destruction and from being brought down by its own strengths. Taken to their logical conclusion, strengths eventually end up as fatal weaknesses. We will always need rescuing from our strengths just as much as from our weaknesses, for unchecked strengths tend to issue in self-destruction. So paradoxical is all of this that you could go so far as to say that altruism constitutes ultimately enlightened self-interest. That, of course, is very much the emphasis that Jesus gives in his teaching: 'Those who want to save their life will lose it, and those who lose their life for my sake will find it' (Matthew 16:25).

A theology of altruism would suggest that it has been there from the dawn of time, implicit in the creative Word of God, 'destined before the foundation of the world' (1 Peter 1:20), increasingly revealed through far-seeing prophets and philosophers, and eventually made explicit on the landscape of history when the Word (Logos) became flesh and we were able to behold the glory of this yet more excellent way of life in our evolving creation.

The great contrast between the ideology of the kingdoms of this world and that of the coming kingdom of God is to be found at just this point. In the world the natural tendency is 'every man for himself', but in the kingdom of God it will ultimately be 'every man for others'. The lifestyle of the 'priest-hood of all believers', as defined by Paul and in the first let-ter of Peter, is exemplified in this willingness to live for others to the point of being ready to die for them if necessary. This should be the way in which the Christian way of life distin-guishes itself from what might simply be called a good life. It is nothing less than that 'new and living way' of which Jesus speaks in his high-priestly prayer in John's Gospel: 'No one has greater love than this, to lay down one's life for one's friends' (John 15:13). Elsewhere he says, 'The Son of Man came not to be served but to serve, and to give his life . . . for many' (Matthew 20:28). This is the distinctive characteristic of what the Bible calls the 'priestly' life, and is a quality of life in which we all share by virtue of our baptismal 'ordination'. Peter reminds the recipients of this letter that they are 'a royal priesthood . . . God's own people' (1 Peter 2:9).

Perhaps it needs to be said in passing that, in speaking of the priesthood of all believers, we do not mean the priesthood of *every* believer. The ordained priesthood is there to focus the essential characteristic of the life of the whole priestly community – that priestly life in which all members of the Body of Christ participate by their baptism. All baptized Christians, however, are called to live the priestly lifestyle in sacrificial service and as 'life for others'.

In the Old Testament, only one of the twelve tribes – the tribe of Aaron – was the priestly tribe, which existed in order to call down God's blessings upon the other eleven tribes. 'Aaron shall bear the names of the sons of Israel in the breast-piece of judgement on his heart when he goes into the holy place, for a continual remembrance before the LORD' (Exodus 28:29). He would carry on his breast a prayer for each of the other eleven tribes, their names engraved on precious stones. The people of God, under the symbol of those gleaming stones, were held up to the light of the Lord in the Holy of Holies in order to be enlightened by him.

Likewise, when Christians come to the Eucharist, they do not pray so much for themselves as for others – including those who are not members of the Church. When the celebrant of the Eucharist says, 'Lift up your hearts,' the priestly community holds up before God those who are on their hearts – those people for whom they care, for whom they pray, for whom they live and for whom, if need be, they might be prepared to die. We call this prayer for others 'intercession', a word which comes from Roman law and which means 'to go before the judge on somebody else's behalf to plead their cause'. In a word, we are 'advocates'. In God's kingdom you do not plead your own cause – you leave somebody else to do that.

Properly understood, however, intercession is not only a way of praying, but a whole new way of living – the revolutionary lifestyle of God's coming kingdom in which it is no longer 'every man for himself', but 'every man for others'. Living for ourselves spells death; living for others opens up endless possibilities for new life. Indeed, new life can only emerge out of life laid down, as we see supremely in Christ's unique offering of himself on the cross, wherein lies the secret of true resurrection. This pattern of life, laid down by the chosen few for the greater good of many others, should be reflected in the life of all God's chosen people. That is what Paul means when he speaks of the vocation of the Christian community to make up 'what is lacking' in the all-sufficient offering of Christ in his life and death for others (see Colossians 1:24).

It is not an exaggeration to see this pattern of intercessory prayer and life at work in the Christian formation of Augustine, who certainly perceived in his *Confessions* the part played in his conversion by his mother's sacrificial life of prayer on his behalf. It is not an overexaggeration, even, to claim that Monica had lived and died for her son. She says as much when she is dying in Ostia, while the group waits for a ship to take them back to North Africa: 'My son, as for myself, I now find no pleasure in this life. What I have still to do here, and why I am here, I do not know. My hope in this world is already fulfilled. The one reason why I wanted to stay longer in this life was my desire to see you a Catholic Christian before I die. My God has granted this in a way more than I had hoped for.'[7] Her whole life was lived for others.

We see this distinctive vocation replicated in the life of many women throughout the ages – arguably more so than in the lives of men. Perhaps that is why we speak of 'mother Church', and perhaps that is also why there have nearly always been more women attending church than men! Is it because, biologically, this model of 'life for others' is distinctively and even instinctively integral to womanhood? In the Bible we see it in the life and vocation of Queen Esther, who went before King Ahasuerus, unsummoned and at the risk of her own life, to plead for the Jews who were being persecuted at the hands of the wicked Haman. Queen Esther demonstrated the core of an intercessory life by going before the king not to plead her own cause, but to plead for her people – regardless of her own safety. Such is the quality and extent of this vocation to 'priestly living' that must distinguish the Christian life from what the world considers to be a good life.

The story of the witness and martyrdom of Maximillian Kolbe during the Second World War demonstrates this distinctive lifestyle in the most poignant way. It was a hot summer's day in the prisoner-of-war camp at Auschwitz. The men had been standing in the courtyard all day long under the blazing sun without anything to eat or drink. The previous evening a prisoner had supposedly escaped. Ten men were to pay the price for this with their lives, by being sent to the starvation bunker. The German commandant strode down into the courtyard in the late afternoon and walked up and down the ranks, pointing arbitrarily to the men who would go to the bunker.

As he came to the third or fourth row, he pointed to a man who immediately broke down and began to weep. 'Oh God, my wife and my children!' he cried.

At that moment a little man wearing spectacles stepped forward. 'May I speak to the German commandant?' he said.

'Yes? What would the Polish pig want to say to the German commandant?'

'Sir, I'm a priest and have no wife and no children. I should like to die in that man's place.'

'Your wish is granted.'

That night nine men and one priest went to the starvation bunker. In such cases the men usually died eating one another, yet on this occasion the men died singing hymns. One of the German officers, giving evidence later at the Nuremburg tribunal, had been given the job of removing the dead bodies. He described how entering the bunker had been like entering a church where the sacrament was reserved, so very powerful was the presence of Christ. Father Maximillian Kolbe was the last to die, and in fact had to be given a lethal injection. The following day they found the body of the supposedly escaped prisoner drowned in a latrine. Had it all been a great waste?

Then, on 19 October 1971, before a crowd of thousands in St Peter's Square in Rome, the Pope recognized the distinctive vocation of Father Kolbe by canonizing him according to the Roman Catholic tradition. Present on that occasion was the prisoner, Franciszek Gajowniczek, then seventy-five years old, who had broken down in the courtyard and in whose place the priest had voluntarily died. He was accompanied by his wife, his children and his children's children, all sitting near the altar for the Mass of Beatification.

THE MANY, THE FEW AND THE ONE

'Many are called, but few are chosen' (Matthew 22:14). God's 'chosen people' are not chosen for privilege, but rather for sacrificial service. It was the failure of the chosen people of Israel to realize their distinctive vocation that led to their spiritual downfall. God's few chosen people are chosen not for their own sakes, but for the sake of the many who are called and do not appear to be responding. The whole human race is called by God to follow Christ, but in every generation only the chosen few respond – God's 'elect'. This is how it works: the many are influenced and saved by the few, just as the few are influenced and saved by the One. Such is the economy of God's plan for the salvation of the world.

'How odd of God to choose the Jews' was a phrase coined by the British writer William Ewer in 1924 – yet how much odder of God to choose people like you and me when there would seem to be so many others much more suited to the task! We need to recall Paul's words to the Corinthians, when he reminded them that not many of them were particularly distinguished by the world's standards when they were first called to be Christians. The mystery of election is a mystery indeed. But as God tells the prophet Samuel, 'The LORD does not see as mortals see; they look on the outward appearance, but the LORD looks on the heart' (1 Samuel 16:7).

It is only as we wrestle with our own sense of vocation that we slowly come to see the wisdom in God's choice. We realize that our own fulfilment (and, indeed, our salvation) is only possible through the service of others – and that perhaps we even *need* to be needed! Sometimes this whole business of vocation turns out to be something of a joke, something vaguely ridiculous. After all, who would have thought that King David could ever become the 'salvation' figure of the Old Testament, prefiguring the true King of the Jews? That is equally true in the New Testament. Who would have thought that foot-in-mouth Peter could ever be chosen as prince of the apostolic band? Surely John was the obvious candidate for that.

There is a very telling passage in Dorothy L. Sayers' *Zeal of Thine House*, a play written for the Canterbury Festival in 1937. The play is all about the construction of Canterbury Cathedral after the choir had been burned down in 1174. The climax of the play comes when Theodatus, the monks' sacristan, goes to the Prior to protest at the morals of the architect, William of Sens. The Prior turns to Theodatus and says,

> Will you not let God manage his own business? My son, he was a carpenter and knows his trade better perhaps than we do, having had some centuries of experience; nor will he, like a bad workman, blame the tools wherewith he builds his city of Zion, here on earth. For God founded his church, not upon John, the loved disciple that lay so close to his heart and knew his mind – not upon John, but Peter; Peter the liar, Peter the coward, Peter the rock, the common man. John was all gold, and gold is rare; the work might wait while God ransacked the corners of the earth to find another John; but Peter is the stone whereof the world is made. So stands the church, stone upon stone, and Christ the cornerstone, with you and me and Peter; and he can, being the alchemist, the stone of Solomon, turn stone to gold and purge the gold itself from dross, till all is gold.[8]

Augustine, like Peter and so many others, found in their vocation the way to their ultimate sanctification, and clearly those whom God chooses are frequently the last people in the world whom the worldly-wise would choose. Yet we are told that, in God's kingdom, the last will be first and the first will be last. As Paul had to learn, 'God chose what is foolish in the world to shame the wise; God chose what is weak in the world to shame the strong' (1 Corinthians 1:27), bringing his strength to perfection in and through our weakness (see 2 Corinthians 5–10). Vocation and election constitute a great mystery in the lives of God's chosen people, but one thing is clear: there can be no boasting on the part of those who have been chosen. 'Let the one who boasts, boast in the Lord' (2 Corinthians 10:17).

Ultimately, this new way of living – the only kind of life that is really worth living – is caught rather than taught. The right people (however few) in the right place at the right time, doing and saying the right things, can make all the difference in the world. A small hinge in the right place will open the massive doors of a fortress. A small rudder will turn a huge ship. In the same way, we might say that the completion of Christ's work for the salvation of the world 'hinges' on God's chosen few, his priestly people, the Body of Christ on earth.

The conversion of the world will not be brought about by a majority, but rather by the strategic placing of the chosen few. That has been God's way since the dawn of time, and he shows no signs of changing his plans for the salvation of the world. A delightful story in the Apocrypha relates how, when Jesus returns to heaven at the Ascension, he and the angels look down at the frail little band of eleven disciples (some still doubting) left behind to complete his mission. The angels simply cannot believe that Jesus is prepared to leave the future of his life's mission in the hands of such a small and unimpressive group. 'Don't you have a further plan?' the angels ask. 'No,' replies Jesus with a quiet confidence. 'I have no other plan.'

DISCIPLESHIP AND VOCATION

As we have seen, whenever and wherever a man or woman is touched by God and sets out on the long road of discipleship, that person needs to know that he or she has been chosen, not for privilege but for sacrificial service. Lose that sense of vocation, and discipleship dies.

Sadly, we tend to speak of vocation to ministry and service in a rather restricted sense these days – in terms of being called to the ordained ministry of the Church. That is only one expression of a Christian's vocation. Instruction in the matters of the Christian faith should enlighten our minds, while worship, prayer and the anointing of the Holy Spirit should warm our hearts. As our discipleship develops, our spiritual journey will bring us to the point where, by the grace of God, our wills are fired as we feel chosen to spend the rest of our lives not merely occupying a space, but making a definitive difference. Making that difference will mean no longer living for ourselves alone. As Jesus warned Peter when he faced him with the full implications of his unique vocation, 'When you were younger, you used to fasten your own belt and to go wherever you wished. But when you grow old, you will stretch out your hands, and someone else will fasten a belt around you and take you where you do not wish to go' (John 21:18).

As we respond as disciples to our particular vocation of service and sacrifice, with both our wills and our hearts, something fundamental is changed. Our works of service are not now undertaken in order to win acceptance with God, or with anybody else for that matter. In the letter to the Ephesians, we read,

> Slaves, obey your earthly masters with fear and trembling, in singleness of heart, as you obey Christ; not only while being watched, and in order to please them, but as slaves

of Christ, doing the will of God from the heart. Render service with enthusiasm, as to the Lord and not to men and women, knowing that whatever good we do, we will receive the same again from the Lord, whether we are slaves or free. (Ephesians 6:5–8)

It is now a matter of knowing in our heart that we have been accepted, and that we are undertaking a life of service in gratitude for the loving acceptance we have received through no virtue of our own. All the distinguished servants of God throughout the ages have only really undertaken a life of joyful service after their hearts have first been overwhelmed with the realization that God has accepted them in Christ by grace. St Paul, Augustine, St Francis, St Clare, John Wesley, Josephine Butler and Mother Teresa are just a few of the figures who spring to mind.

Justification leads into vocation, which in turn is part and parcel of our ultimate sanctification. *Justification* is that action of God by which he chooses to wipe the slate clean and to give us a totally fresh start. We appropriate this wonderful gift and make it our own by reaching out with both hands to Christ in faith and trust. *Vocation* is God's tailor-made and personalized way of life that harnesses our particular strengths and weaknesses in the service of God and of others. *Sanctification* is the lifelong process of becoming increasingly what, by justification, we already are – children of God, reflecting uniquely some aspect of God's own character. Our vocation is the means by which we are sanctified. This process is experienced by many as the phenomenon John Wesley described as a 'strange warming of the heart', which eventually fires the will to live for others, even to the point of being prepared to die for them. Augustine summarized it in one of his immortal phrases: 'Oh God, grant that I may love what you will and will what you love.'

We do not reach this point in our spiritual journey in the first five minutes, however. It is sometimes only in old age, when we can no longer do what we used to be able to do, that we can be still enough to fulfil an intercessory way of life through means of prayer for others. This ministry of intercessory prayer is often given to the housebound, for example, who have both time and space in their lives to take others on board, to hold them before God in their hearts in extended times of intercessory prayer. This ministry is just as much (if not more) for laypeople as for the ordained priest. One old and godly priest wrote in his annual Advent letter that, although he would try to continue doing what he had done over the years of his active ministry, he sensed that 'gradually there will be more "space" to embrace the world on one's knees'.

It is more than just a play on words to recall the root meaning of the name Joshua or Jesus. Joshua means 'the one who saves'. Donald Coggan goes deeper into this meaning when he says,

> Here was an idea whose roots went deep down into Jewish soil. Jesus – Joshua – deliverance *from* and *to* . . . The name which is above every name is derived from a Hebrew root that denotes 'to be spacious'. In other words a 'salvation' figure is someone who has space for others precisely because they are not full of themselves. They are not simply occupying a space but rather making a difference by *offering* their space for others – by making space in their hearts and in their lives. That is very much a Jesus and 'salvation' characteristic. John the Baptist was a case in point when he said of Jesus that 'he must increase, I must decrease'. And again as Paul reminds us: 'Jesus did not grasp at equality with God, but emptied himself.[9]

That is why there is room in Jesus' heart for his people, so that he can live for ever and make intercession before God for us. Moreover, God is searching for men and women with enough space in their hearts for others – men and women who can join with Christ in his saving, intercessory work for the whole world.

In the kingdoms of this world, where it is so clearly a matter of 'every man for himself', in an age of heightened individualism, we increasingly speak of people 'invading our space'. In the kingdom of God, where it will be 'every man for others', God's chosen men and women offer to others the hospitality of space in their hearts and lives, because they have first offered that prayer from the heart: 'O come to my heart, Lord Jesus, make space and room in my heart and my life for Thee.'

By the end of AD 388, Augustine found that following the deaths of his mother, his son and his close friend, not even the little community around him was enough to fill his life and his heart. Called from the life of academia, he now needed to discover what he had been called to and for. He made his discoveries by what many would dismiss as a series of accidents, but which, with the value of hindsight, he would come to see as part of the same loving Providence that had first touched his life in the garden through the reading of Scripture some years earlier. To borrow from G.K. Chesterton once more, what Augustine had at first thought to be a 'resting place', with his little community, suddenly became 'a pub', now urgently pointing back to the road and to his continuing spiritual journey. As Augustine himself poignantly said, 'The man journeying to his own country must not mistake the inn for his home.'[10]

QUESTIONS FOR FURTHER REFLECTION

Prayer of St Augustine

What tortuous ways I walked! Woe to that rash soul of mine, that hoped by abandoning you, Lord, to find something better! It tossed and turned upon its back, upon its sides, upon its belly, yet it found every place it lay to be hard – you alone Lord are my rest. And behold, you are near at hand, and you deliver us from our wretched wonderings, and you settle us in your own way. And you comfort us, saying: 'Run, I will carry you; yes, I will lead you to the end of your journey, and there also I will carry you.' Amen.

For personal reflection

1. On page 151 you read the phrase 'paralysis of analysis'. Is this something that has trapped you or someone you know? Weigh up the dangers of getting stuck at either extreme of the spectrum, either where all is reflection with no activity, or where all is service with no reflection. Have there been periods of imbalance in your life? Mark them on your time line. Where do you tend to stay on the spectrum?

2. 'Our distinctive vocation to service is the means by which God styles our ultimate sanctification' (see page 153). What does this mean to you, and how has it worked out in your experience?

3. 'We will always need rescuing from our strengths just as much as from our weaknesses, for unchecked strengths tend to issue in self-destruction' (see page 154). What are your strengths? What danger could each lead you into? Do you agree with this statement?

4. Jesus left the future of his life's mission with a small and unimpressive group of disciples. Is there any part of God's purposes for which you feel he is relying on you? Do you feel resentful or proud that this might be so?

5. The powerful story of the sacrifice of Maximillian Kolbe (see page 157) affects people in different ways. Do you feel sad, angry, humble or uplifted? Imagine that you meet him in heaven: what would he say about himself, and what would you want to say to him?

For group discussion

1. Read James 1:22–7. Relate this passage to your answers to Questions 1, 4 and 5 above. In the light of the passage, what will you do with the insights you have gained about your spiritual walk by following this book?

2. Work through the questions for personal reflection together with the group, in so far as you feel able.

3. How do you react to the idea of intercession as a way of life? Do you know anyone who exemplifies this for you? Is it a goal you would seek to attain?

Bible passage for meditation

We have thought a great deal about moving on and growing spiritually. Paul's prayer sums up what he saw to be the essence of spiritual growth. As you breathe in the breadth of his vision, pray it for yourself, for the members of the group, and for others whom you wish to remember in your prayers.

Ephesians 3:14

For this reason I bow my knees before the Father . . . that, according to the riches of his glory, he may grant that you may be strengthened in your inner being with power through his Spirit, and that Christ may dwell in your hearts through faith, as you are being rooted and grounded in love. I pray that you may . . . know the love of Christ that surpasses knowledge, so that you may be filled with all the fullness of God.

SIX

The Point of It All

> Not that I have already obtained this or have already reached the goal; but I press on to make it my own, because Christ Jesus has made me his own. Beloved, I do not consider that I have made it my own; but this one thing I do: forgetting what lies behind and straining forward to what lies ahead, I press on toward the goal for the prize of the heavenly call of God in Christ Jesus.
>
> *Philippians 3:12–14*

St Augustine wrote,

Spiritual renewal is not accomplished in one moment of conversion, in which our sins are forgiven. After all, it is one thing to recover from a fever, but quite another to regain one's health after it. It is one thing to remove a spear from a wound, but quite another for the wound to heal completely. So to begin the cure we remove the cause of the sickness, and this occurs through the forgiveness of our sins. Then there follows the process of healing: 'our inner man is renewed from day to day', as the Apostle said. To be thus renewed by daily progress in the knowledge, justice and holiness of God is to be converted from the temporal to the eternal and from the carnal to the spiritual. Our success in this depends entirely on God, for 'without me you can do nothing'.[1]

Health is a process we undergo, not a product we can acquire. Christian discipleship is, as we have seen, a lengthy process and a long journey from baptism to the vision of God, when we will truly love God with our whole being – heart, mind, soul and strength. Every dynamic within us will be pointing in the same direction, pressing on towards him who made us his own in our baptism (see Philippians 3:12). Throughout this process we need to be looking constantly to Jesus, 'the Author and Perfecter of our faith', and the joy that is set before us on the other side of all our strivings and restlessness.

As disciples we are seeking the city – the New Jerusalem – whose foundations are Christ. The foundations of that city can never be shaken, and therein lies the nature of Christian hope. Christian hope is certainly not a kind of bland optimism, a vain hope that 'everything will come out in the wash'. When Dame Julian of Norwich exclaimed, 'All shall be well, and all shall be well, and all manner of things shall be well,'[2] she meant the same as Paul did when he said that 'all things work together for good for those who love God, who are called according to his purpose' (Romans 8:28). It is only because of the resurrection and ascension of Christ that our future as Christians is assured: it is not left to chance. The writer of Hebrews described Christians as having 'this hope, a sure and steadfast anchor of the soul' (Hebrews 6:19). Theologians call this a 'realized eschatology': we are living with 'the end in the middle', as Bishop John Robinson put it. The anchor of our redemption no longer tethers us from behind, from the port of our departure. From the time of our baptism, even while we are still at sea, we are tethered from the front to the harbour of our destination, in so far as we are bonded with Christ who has gone ahead to 'prepare a place' for us (John 14:2).

THE END IN THE MIDDLE

At the outset of his long journey of faith, Augustine had declared that it was the very nature of the human condition that our hearts would always be restless until we had come to rest totally in God. Much later in his pilgrimage, when he was a bishop, he wrote these reassuring words: 'Even while we are being tossed about by the waves of the sea, we have the anchor of hope already fixed upon the land.'[3] Augustine lived in this world in the sure and confident hope that the day would come when faith would become sight, when desire would be swallowed up in delight, when the things that could be shaken off would be shaken off for ever, and when all that remained would be the One who remains for ever. Nothing less, he now knew, was worth living for, and nothing less constituted a life worth living.

We might say that in middle life Augustine became 'homesick for heaven' and experienced a deep desire and yearning which overtook his earlier, more negative restlessness. He had discovered, if you like, 'the point of it all' – sometimes summed up in the words, 'In the end, God'. In Chapter 1 we looked at the relative importance of archaeology, the study of where we have come from, and teleology, the study of where we are going. Surely it is far more vital to look forward, to know what our ultimate destination will be. When we reach our true end – the reason for which we were created – we shall be 'perfect' (*teleios* in Greek), not in a perfectionist sense, but rather in the sense that we shall have become who we were originally created to be. The commandment of Jesus, 'Be perfect . . . as your heavenly Father is perfect' (Matthew 5:48) has nothing whatever to do with perfectionism. A proper understanding of this commandment could be paraphrased: 'In the end, become who you truly are and who you were uniquely created to be, just as God is uniquely and truly himself as God.'

Until that point in our long journey of faith, our true identity will remain a mystery, for holiness and wholeness are primarily the grace of God at work in us. We cannot, and should not, style our own holiness. 'We are God's children now,' says John. 'What we will be has not yet been revealed. What we do know is this: when he is revealed, we will be like him' (1 John 3:2). We will be like him, because 'we will see him as he is', and our true identity is known only by the One in whose mind and heart we were first conceived.

We should be cautious, therefore, about simply replacing the word 'holiness' with the more secular words 'wholeness' or 'fulfilment'. Holiness is a fascinating, mysterious and miraculous blending of nature and grace, and is never achieved by us trying to pull ourselves up by our own moral bootstraps. It is God who raises us up at the last to become what he intends us to be, and in that process the work of grace perfects nature but does not annihilate it, to use the words of Thomas Aquinas. Even more fascinating, perhaps, is the discovery that what we had initially regarded as our disastrous weaknesses can turn out to be remarkable, God-given strengths – but always by grace and by grace alone.

St Camillus de Lellis (1550–1614) is a case in point. Born late in the life of his mother, he grew to be a huge man – six foot, six inches tall – and at the age of seventeen went off with his father to fight the Turks. He soon developed an incurable disease of the legs, however, which was to afflict him for the rest of his life. Quarrelsome and difficult in every way, he was thrown out of the hospital for incurables in Rome. By the age of twenty-four he had become a compulsive gambler and had gambled away every penny he owned, all his possessions and finally, on the streets of Naples, even the shirt off his back. He took work as a labourer with the Capuchin Fathers at Manfredonia in 1574, and the following year underwent a dramatic conversion. On the feast of Candlemas, 1575, the Capuchin Father Guardian spoke with Camillus about the state of his soul. Ruminating on the priest's words as he rode away, Camillus was suddenly and forcefully struck with the power of what he had just heard. He fell from his horse with tears of repentance.

Although Camillus wished to enter the Capuchin Order as a novice, his diseased leg prevented this, so he returned to the Hospital of St Giacomo in Rome where he had formerly been such a disagreeable patient. This time, however, he devoted himself as a nurse to the care of the sick, and eventually became superintendent of the hospital. Later he founded an order of companions who worked every day at the great Hospital of the Holy Spirit in Rome. In 1585, living in a larger house to accommodate his growing community, Camillus arranged for his congregation of nurses to serve people infected with the plague, as well as prisoners and those dying in private houses. Towards the end of the century, some of his companions were sent with the troops to Hungary and Croatia on the first recorded military field ambulance service. Camillus, although suffering from serious ill health, lived to see the foundation of fifteen houses of his brothers and eight hospitals in Rome, Naples and farther afield. He was a pioneer in insisting on fresh air and suitable diets for his patients, and the isolation of those with infectious diseases. Canonized the following century, he is rightly and significantly regarded as the patron saint of nurses and the sick. Yes, indeed, out of weakness he was made strong.

Holiness is not like having a moral or spiritual facelift. Rather, it is God at work in our hearts and lives in ways of which we are not even remotely aware. The whole process works best, in fact, when we are not conscious of it and are not looking at ourselves. Continual spiritual renewal occurs when we are looking at God in worship, praise and adoration.

We shall only know who we were uniquely created to be as we come to know the God who created us. We can only become who we are in relationship, not in isolation – in relationship, that is, with God and with others through him. We do not discover our unique identity by looking in a mirror; there is nothing narcissistic about this kind of self-knowledge. Neither shall we discover our true and unique identity through introspection. This kind of knowledge comes through relationship, through the language of love, so eloquently and poetically spelt out in Paul's song to love in 1 Corinthians 13. By grace and grace alone, this amazing scholar of the law finally came to see something of the point of it all when he wrote,

> If I . . . understand all mysteries and all knowledge . . . but do not have love, I am nothing . . . Love never ends . . . As for knowledge, it will come to an end. For we know only in part . . . but when the complete comes, the partial will come to an end . . . For now we see in a mirror, dimly, but then we will see face to face. Now I know only in part; then I will know fully, even as I have been fully known.

This knowledge comes, if you like, from the side of the brain which does not deal with information. In earlier ages, we did not speak of 'the two sides of the brain'. Rather, we designated the 'heart' as that part of ourselves which gained this alternative knowledge through love and loving. To put it another way, inspiration supplements, complements and ultimately transcends mere information.

In our age of information technology, the information side of knowledge is clearly on overdrive, with the awesome possibility that the heart will be sorely neglected with its capacity for adoration, wonder and worship. We have all become victims of the ghastly and distorted legacy of Descartes, who persuaded several successive generations that our humanity could be summarized in that well-known phrase, 'Cogito, ergo sum' – 'I think therefore I am'. Nothing could be further from the truth, yet since the Enlightenment many have become prisoners of their finite minds while at the same time knowing in their hearts that there is so much more out there that can never be reached through cerebral processes. Little wonder that many people seek that further knowledge through self-transcendence in the use of drug-induced hallucinations. Kenneth Leech writes,

> While the drug cultures (for there are a range of them, not one) have changed and expanded, for many young people they still remain a major form of ritual, ecstasy, and what must, without exaggeration, be called spiritual experience. The 'rave' is for many a new form of church, a place of 'ecstasy' – the choice of name for this most popular amphetamine derivative is not accidental – and of temporary transcendence of the conventional. Drugs seem to offer a way of losing oneself, of letting go, of experiencing that wildness and freedom, that sense of the 'beyond' which religion once offered.[4]

In the end, of course, this offers no authentic or lasting solution for the human dilemma. The aim of true self-transcendence is not to *bypass* the mind (which is what drugs achieve), but rather to transcend it through wonder, imagination and worship. (It is not insignificant that the Harry Potter books, which speak to the imagination rather than the intellect, have recently become so popular, not only with children but also for the childlike of heart. That, of course, has been true of all the great so-called 'children's books' throughout the ages.)

Sadly, we live in an age that is in serious danger of losing its capacity for wonder – the ability to stand and stare, the sense of expectation, the heightened awareness of the numinous in the world around us and within us. There is surely an urgent need today to reclaim and recapture this capacity for wonder, within the total understanding of what it is to be truly human. To gain the whole technological world with its vast information resources at the expense of our ability to stop and wonder could well prove to be the ultimate impoverishment of the human spirit. It was Dag Hammarskjöld who wrote in his personal journal, 'God does not die on the day when we cease to believe in a personal deity, but we die on the day when our lives cease to be illumined by the steady radiance, renewed daily, of a wonder, the source of which is beyond all reason.'[5]

Part of the irresistible attraction of newly born babies, when you look into their eyes, is what one author calls 'the new-minted wonder of childhood'. G.K. Chesterton wrote, 'At the back of our brains, so to speak [he might just as easily have said 'at the other side of our brain' or 'in our heart of hearts'], there is a forgotten blaze or burst of astonishment at our own existence. The object of the artistic and spiritual life is to dig for this sunrise of wonder.' Michael Mayne, Dean Emeritus of Westminster Abbey, took those words of Chesterton for the title of a book – *This Sunrise of Wonder* – in which he addressed twenty-four letters to his grandchildren, urging them to cherish and develop their capacity to wonder in an age when this will become an increasingly rare commodity. John Wesley saw the three essential ingredients at the heart of our humanity as 'wonder, love and praise', all converging at that point of full-blooded worship and adoration. Yes, as George Herbert wrote, 'Above all, the heart must bear the longest part.'

The spiritual journey of Henri J.M. Nouwen is of particular interest from this point of view. In his early years he pursued quite a successful academic career, and taught at the prestigious Harvard University. Towards the end of his life, however, he 'dried up'. After a considerable struggle, he found himself – his true self – as a member of the L'Arche Community. In that community was a very seriously handicapped young man called Adam. Nouwen drew closer and closer to Adam in the closing years of his life, and he wrote,

> Somehow during the centuries we have come to believe that what makes us human is our mind ... Adam keeps revealing to me, over and over again and in his own clear way, that what makes us human is not primarily our minds, but our hearts; it is not first of all our ability to think which gives us our particular identity in creation, but it is our ability to love. The one who sees Adam first as a disabled person misses the sacred mystery that Adam is fully capable of receiving and offering love ... Let me say here that by 'heart' I do not mean the seat of human emotions in contrast to the mind as the seat of human thought. No, by heart I mean the centre of our being where God comes to dwell with us and bring us the divine gifts of trust, hope and love. The mind tries to understand, grasp problems, discern different aspects of reality, and probe the mysteries of life. The heart allows us to enter into relationships and experience that we are sons and daughters of God and of our parents, as well as brothers and sisters of one another. Long before our minds were able to exercise their potential, our hearts were developing trusting human relationships. And in fact I am convinced that these trusting human relationships even precede the moment of our birth.[6]

In the fourth century there was a whole school of theology – the Cappadocian Fathers – who pursued this way of knowledge by love, prayer and worship. They fully appreciated the dangers of seeking to know God simply through the mind and the intellect. The temptation of knowledge solely through the mind is the temptation to make God in our own finite images and to back this up with quotations from theological books and Scripture. The seduction of such knowledge is powerful, but in the end it is blasphemous. How can we, with our finite minds, conceive the infinite without in the end committing idolatry? Thus, throughout history, the Eastern Churches have supplemented and complemented the dogmatic theology of the Western Churches with what is called apophatic theology. That is to say, they would claim that it is never possible to say what God is like, only to say what he is not like, because what he is like is totally beyond our imaginings. Towards the end of his life, Augustine summed up his theological experience in these words: 'We can know what God is not, but mortals cannot know what God is.'

Catholic, Protestant and Reformed traditions in the West have all gone astray theologically on this very point. Dogmatic theology coming largely or exclusively from the stable of the intellect, the lecture room, the library and books will always go astray, unless it is supplemented in the laboratory of worship, prayer, wonder and contemplation. The Western Churches have tended to be suspicious of this route, however, seeing it as the very opposite of a discipleship that is involved with the world and its needs – 'the social conscience', as we sometimes call it. In recent history many Christians in the West have viewed the contemplative life as a way of escape from the needs and concerns of the world, the poor and deprived. So they have polarized the life of prayer and worship and the active life of serving the needs of the world. Yet they have failed to wrestle with the fact that history conclusively shows that this shallow thesis is the very opposite of the truth. For it is the contemplatives – St John of the Cross, Mother Teresa, Thomas Merton and Henri Nouwen, to name but a few – who have found the way from the heart to the will. It is the contemplatives who have discovered that worship and wonder open us up to powerful mission and compassionate ministry both to and for the world. William Temple, the great social-activist archbishop of the twentieth century, rightly claimed that 'the world can be saved from political chaos and collapse by one thing only, and that is worship.'[7]

I WORSHIP, THEREFORE I AM

Let us turn back to the most fundamental question of all, with which Augustine wrestled from the outset of his spiritual journey: 'Why was I created?' In the Westminster Catechism, the response to the question, 'To what end was I created?' is very simple: 'I was created in order to worship God and to enjoy him for ever.' If that reply is true, then it has huge significance for the whole basis of the human condition, not simply the Christian calling. If it is true, then until we discover, experience and pursue true and authentic worship, we shall be less than human, for worship is the fundamental instinct within every creature, an instinct far more basic and a drive far more powerful even than that of our sexuality. Nevertheless, this instinctive drive to worship seems to be scarcely heeded in the ordinary daily conversation and concerns of the twenty-first century – and is positively neglected in the syllabus of contemporary education.

'If you don't worship you'll shrink: it's as brutal as that,' remarks the psychiatrist in Peter Shaffer's play *Equus*. Like all basic human instincts, if the instinct to worship is neglected, frustrated or suppressed, it does not disappear. Neglected or misdirected worship develops the power to corrupt and even destroy, simply because humanity, which was made for worship, will demand ways of expressing this compulsive drive in one form or another – for good or ill. Either we turn to drug-induced 'ecstasy', or we attach our need for worship to something or somebody less than worthy of our honour.

Make no mistake about it: whenever we begin to worship and whatever we begin to worship, both are capable of resulting in the best or the worst. We are taken over by what we worship, we identify with it, we fall in love with it and cannot do without it. In other words, we surrender our freedom in compulsive patterns of behaviour. Taken to extremes, we lose our freedom and find ourselves in bondage to objects or persons who could never fulfil us, however much we have of them. Alcoholism, gambling, drug addiction and erotomania are commonplace compulsions today. False gods lead to a loss of freedom; the one true and living God will lead us into freedom, as far as we can bear it.

Truth to tell, we were not born to be free; we were born to be possessed! This is why false worship (or idolatry) is at the heart of most of our contemporary ills. In our materialistic, self-centred world, we run the grave risk of being possessed either by our possessions or ourselves, caught up in a narcissistic drive to look no further than the mirror and our own image. Yes, the claim that we were created to be free is more of an illusion than a reality. Our true freedom, paradoxically, lies precisely in our need to be possessed. Augustine rightly claims, having proved his thesis through experience, that only when we are totally possessed by God through worshipping him do we find our true freedom – in God, 'whose service [bondage] is perfect freedom'. That is also Paul's thesis in Romans: humanity, he claims, has 'exchanged the truth about God for a lie and worshipped and served the creature rather than the Creator' (Romans 1:25). It is not unrealistic, therefore, to claim that the opposite of sin is not virtue but worship of the one true God. Sin is essentially misdirected worship, and virtue is the worship of God in and above all things – the God who alone is worthy of our worship.

Clearly not all worship is good or true: we need to learn to worship as surely as we have to learn to do properly what at first came to us by instinct. What a child at first does by nature has to be relearned if it is to 'stand up' in the adult world. The instinct to worship needs to be directed if it is not to be corrupted. Every political tyrant since the dawn of history has recognized the power of worship and the compulsive need within every human being to express this instinct and find objects for worship. When this instinct to worship is wrongly directed, there are scarcely any limits to the depravity to which the human race can sink. The twentieth century was strewn with the wreckage of what happens when religion goes wrong – from the crimes of Nazism to the mass suicide of the People's Temple in Guyana in 1979; from the events in Waco, Texas, in 1994 to the chemical warfare in Tokyo's subway in 1995 – and all undertaken in the name of religion by compulsive, obsessive personalities fired up by the worship of a corrupt leader. Thus Colin Dunlop writes,

> A man may divert his powers of worship away from God and set it upon himself or even upon the State. For people who know nothing about the true God, or who, though knowing God, are not interested in him, may still worship. For the fact that such worship is not directed to its true end does not prevent it being real worship. But worship of what is less than God, or opposed to God, though real, is harmful. Therefore it is essential that man learn to worship the true God and to give his homage where it rightly

belongs. For to worship is to acknowledge with every part of one's being the worthship of what is worshipped, to acknowledge with the mind, the affections and the will its utter perfection. To commit oneself thus towards what is imperfect or perishable is to engender the lie in the soul; while thus to render homage to what objectively claims it, namely Almighty God, is to take one's appointed place in the universe and to do what each of us was born to do.[8]

There was a time when religion and learning went hand in hand. The ancient universities were all known originally as places of 'religion and learning', constituting an environment in which mind, heart and will were pointing in the same direction. Indeed, the layout of an Oxford or Cambridge college still resembles that of an ancient Benedictine monastery, with the architectural plan making explicit what is required for us to become fully and truly human: eating and drinking together in the great hall, living in collegiality around a garden and frequently beside a river, taking tutorials together within the college, and, at the heart of it all, attending worship services in the chapel.

In such places and in such an environment, education and discernment – the mind, the heart and the spirit – are all pursued together, and all this is set within a community in which belonging, believing and behaving are nurtured in daily worship . . . In such places worshippers met in buildings where architecture and design invited the healthy experience of the transcendent. In such environments heart and mind could grow together. Worship was informed by truth and moral commitment; scholarship was lifted beyond itself into the fuller environment of adoration.[9]

In the light of all this, it should by now be self-evident that all ordained ministers, priests and pastors urgently need to be recalled to their primary task of ministering to the religious needs of people and to this primary instinct to worship. Such a ministry is surely just as much a skill as it is a charism – a talent as well as a gift. All gifts require discipline and practice, just as skills do – like the gift of music-making, for example. They have to be learned, and in the case of ministry the curriculum should include everything from Christian formation and spiritual direction to learning how (and how not) to lead worship in ways that will open doors for ordinary people onto a larger, transcendent world and an enriched life, while constantly feeding those committed to their care with the Word of God and the sacraments of the Church. We need this most urgently today. Lost in a labyrinth of false religious alternatives, in a supermarket of pick-and-mix options not dissimilar to that of Augustine's day, our own age is crying out to be shown a way to the truth and to the warmth of the sunshine – the 'sunrise of wonder'. Moonshine is certainly no substitute! W.H. Auden was prophetic as well as poetic when he wrote,

> In the deserts of the heart
> Let the healing fountain start
> In the prison of his days
> Teach the freeman how to praise.[10]

WORSHIP AND LIFE

Transcendence transforms. We become what we worship. In Luke's account of the transfiguration, we read the moving verse, 'While he [Jesus] was praying, the appearance of his face changed' (Luke 9:29). Even in hero worship, the worshippers often take on something of their hero's mannerisms or style – something 'rubs off' from the hero to the worshipper. In true and authentic worship, we are most surely changed. Indeed, perhaps it should be made clearer to churchgoers that their attendance at worship automatically presupposes their willingness to be changed, 'from one degree of glory to another' (2 Corinthians 3:18). Irenaeus wrote, 'The glory of God is a human being fully alive: and the glory of our humanity is the vision of God.' That is precisely what guarantees John's thesis in his first epistle that, when we finally see God, 'we will be like him' (1 John 3:2). Holiness of life is never achieved by being self-conscious or simply striving to be more 'Christlike'. Such a life is not a copy or imitation of Christ's life, but rather a reflection of it, and this will happen most truly when we are not aware of it, as we become increasingly 'lost in wonder, love and praise'. Unless we can lose ourselves, we will never discover our true selves.

I like to think that the so-called 'Toronto blessing' and, indeed, the whole charismatic movement, which has brought so many blessings to the Church, was given for such a time as this – a time of emotional aridity. Frequently on this long journey from head to heart to will, moments will occur when 'something has to give'. Inhibitions inflicted by parents, friends, society or bad religious teaching (among other things) will restrict our capacity to let go and let God pick us up and transform us in the intimacy of his loving embrace. G.K. Chesterton said, 'The madman is not the man who has lost his reason, but rather the man who has lost everything except his reason.' The madness of the post-Enlightenment era has been crying out for some time to be released from the prison of ideas and information, facts and figures, into the realm of inspiration and imagination.

That is not to say that Christianity should promote a mindless religion – far from it. Nor is it necessarily wise to move out of the driving seat – to surrender control – unless you can be quite certain that the One who replaces you in the driving seat of your will is a proven and skilled driver. Of course there is risk, infinite risk, in all of this. Nonetheless, the Holy Spirit, breathed into us in worship, can 'blow us gently where he wills', bending our own stubborn wills to the gentle rule of his love. With this wind in our sails, we move along the road of discipleship and development, breaking through the inhibitions which are holding us back and being released into authentic self-transcendence. In this way, self-consciousness is overtaken by self-transcendence.

Henri Nouwen describes in one of his many writings how he came to know the trapeze artists in a circus which came for a while to perform close to where he was living. The trapeze artists told him about their skills. Apparently, if you are a trapeze artist you are either a 'thrower' or a 'catcher', and the essential rule is that the thrower must never try to catch the catcher. Rather, the thrower must launch into the jump with that total abandonment and trust which refuses to grasp at the catcher. To grasp is almost certainly to miss and fall, or even to break the arms of the waiting catcher.

Such is the integrity of true Christian discipleship with its call to self-abandonment – the self-abandonment at the heart of all faith and love. Faith, or trust (in many ways a better word in the context of Christian discipleship), is inevitably bound up with risk. The Scriptures give us a paradoxically double injunction: 'Resist not the Spirit,' yet also, 'Test the spirits to see whether they are of God,' for we must remember that the devil also has his charismatics! One of the tests of authentic worship is whether it is truly holistic, in the sense that it brings every aspect of our being into line and on target. William Temple wrote,

> To worship is to quicken the conscience by the holiness of God, to feed the mind with the truth of God, to purge the imagination by the beauty of God, to open the heart to the love of God, to devote the will to the purpose of God. All this is gathered up in that emotion which most cleanses us from selfishness because it is the most selfless of all emotions – adoration.[11]

This is precisely what should be taking place every Sunday morning in every church, when disciples gather together for worship and to take on fuel for the longest journey in the world.

WORSHIP AND SERVICE

What happens when worship is finished (at the church service, that is, because in one sense worship never ends)? To quote William Temple again: 'Worship includes all life and the moments spent in concentrated worship, whether in church or elsewhere, are the focusing points of the sustaining and directing energy of the worshipper's whole life.'[12] The cliché which runs, 'When the worship is ended the service begins,' should bring us all up with a start, for it presents us with two remarkable challenges. The first challenge is the refusal to lock God up in his churches, in the specific places set aside for worship. The second challenge, presented to us at all the most unlikely moments, is that whenever and wherever we discover the presence of God, our response will be one of loving service – in the high street as much as in the sanctuary.

> Teach me my God and King
> In all things thee to see,
> And what I do in anything
> To do it as for Thee.

In this well-known hymn, the Anglican priest and poet George Herbert catches the vision of holistic worship in its fullest sense. It is his prayer, as it should be the prayer of every disciple, that once we have found God in special places and at special times set aside for worship, we will go on to discover his loving presence in the whole universe, just as Isaiah was instructed to do in his vision in the Temple. In the Temple the seraphs called to one another, saying, 'Holy, holy, holy is the LORD of hosts; the whole earth is full of his glory' (Isaiah 6:3).

Disciples of Christ are intended to go out from formal worship to discover, recover and uncover that same glory, with eyes that have had their perspective radically refocused by the specific encounter of eucharistic and sacramental worship. True worship should issue in mission. Worship that does not issue in wider service is not worthy of the name of Christian worship. Speaking of caring for the hungry, thirsty, lonely, needy, sick and imprisoned, Jesus says, 'Truly I tell you, just as you did it to one of the least of these who are members of my family, you did it to me' (Matthew 25:40). It is worth noticing how worship issues in mission once again in the concluding chapter of Matthew's Gospel. We are told that the disciples 'worshipped' Jesus on top of the mountain, and then were immediately given the great missionary commandment, 'Go therefore and make disciples . . .' (Matthew 28:19).

Ultimately, worship in the sanctuary and service in the world are not in opposition. John Wesley said, 'There is no holiness but social holiness,' and Dag Hammarskjöld insisted, 'The road to holiness necessarily passes through the world of action.' As worshippers, we need to recall constantly and daily that the God whom we worship and serve in the sanctuary is the same God whom we worship and serve in the slum.

The Christian socialist movement in the late nineteenth century in England was much inspired by what we would probably call 'high church' worship, while the Clapham Sect, involving such people as the anti-slave-trade campaigner William Wilberforce, was influenced by strong evangelical preaching for conversion. Yet it was Christ who gave, and who continues to give, both Church traditions a common concern for the poor and needy. It was only a later distortion of the gospel to see worship and the social gospel as opposites or, worse still, as options we can choose according to our preferences and whims. At the Anglo-Catholic Congress of 1923, Bishop Weston of Zanzibar challenged the Church with the following words from his address, entitled 'Our Present Duty':

> You are Christians?
> Then your Lord is one and the same
> with Jesus on the throne of his glory,
> with Jesus in his blessed sacrament,
> with Jesus received in your hearts in Communion
> with Jesus who is mystically with you as you pray,
> and with Jesus enshrined in the hearts and bodies
> of his brothers and sisters up and down the world.
>
> Now go out into the highways and hedges,
> and look for Jesus in the ragged and the naked,
> in the oppressed and the sweated, in those who have
>   lost hope
> and in those who are struggling to make good.
> Look for Jesus in them; and when you find him,
> gird yourselves with his towel of fellowship,
> and wash his feet in the person of his brethren.

In the end it is all a matter of making the connection between the Body of Christ in the Communion service and the same Body of Christ in the community of the poor, the needy and those who, in the words of the first beatitude, have come to know their need of God, so that 'God is all in all'. On the road to Damascus, the voice heard by Paul accuses him not of persecuting Christians, but of persecuting Christ: 'Saul, Saul, why do you persecute me?' (Acts 9:4) Yes, for good or ill, 'just as you did it to the least of these who are members of my family, you did it to me.' That is essentially the gospel connection between worship and service – they are both different sides of the same coin of love.

A HOLY DEATH

The consummation of a holy life of worship and service must surely be a holy death, as the ultimate offering to God of ourselves, our souls and our bodies. In contrast to the prevailing secular attitude of our world today, which consistently expresses the desire for a quick death, the Christian, in the words of the Litany, prays to be delivered 'from sudden death'. For the man or woman of faith, death is part of the great journey of faith, part of the greater offering of a life of discipleship. The invitation of Jesus to follow him includes following him through life *and* death, to that greater life beyond. If Jesus is our companion on the journey through this life, then he will continue to be our companion and guide through death to the life beyond, where he has made preparations for us. Given the chance, therefore, the Christian will want time to prepare for a holy death.

As Augustine lay dying in the summer of AD 430, Roman rule in Africa was collapsing. It was the end of a civilization which, when Augustine was born, would have been taken for granted to have lasted for a thousand years. In the winter of AD 429 the Vandals surrounded the town of Hippo. Their fleet held the sea. According to his biographer Possidius, in the last months of his life Augustine saw

> whole cities sacked, country villas razed, their owners killed or scattered as refugees, the churches deprived of their bishops and clergy . . . some tortured to death, some killed outright, others as prisoners, reduced to losing their integrity, in soul and body, to serve an evil and brutal enemy. The hymns of God and praises in the churches had come to a stop. In many places the church-buildings were burnt to the ground; the sacrifices of God could no longer be celebrated in their proper place, and the divine sacraments were either not sought, or, when sought, no one could be found to give them.[13]

In those last months, Augustine seems to have remained very active in mind and body, ministering faithfully in a church packed with the demoralized flock of a once-splendid Roman society, watching as his life's work was destroyed before his very eyes. Yet he was preparing his will, and had set about revising and editing the vast number of his writings, which were to be his great bequest to future generations of Christians. He was setting his house in order, if you like.

In what he called his *Retractions,* he revised his lifetime's books, letters and sermons in such a way that future generations of readers would be able to appreciate the long journey of mind and heart that he had taken to reach his ultimate goal. On that journey Augustine had changed, and he was not ashamed to accept the fact that he would not write in the year AD 430 quite the same things as he wrote at the outset of his Christian discipleship. He might well have agreed with the words John Henry Newman wrote so many years later: 'To live is to change and to be perfect is to have changed often.' This is why the writings in his *Retractions* are no longer arranged in subject order but rather in chronological order, tracing the development of his maturity on that long journey from head to heart, and from heart to will. The *Retractions* represent Augustine's theological repentance, that constant reviewing of the situation that had been a consistent characteristic of his lifetime's journey of faith. In August AD 430, Augustine fell ill with a severe fever which proved to be terminal. He died and was buried on 28 August.

The last great work that occupied Augustine's energies in the concluding years of his life and ministry was *De Civitate Dei*, 'The City of God'. It is a massive work and took him many years to write. As it draws to a conclusion, rather like the last book in the Bible, our eyes begin to look heavenwards to that new Jerusalem and to the eternal worship of heaven. Augustine's concluding words, addressed just as much to his own restless heart as to the restless and violent world in which he lived (not so different from our own), are designed to share with us a glimpse of that greater worship, the worship of heaven in the heavenly city: 'Then we shall be still and we shall see, we shall see and we shall love, we shall love and we shall praise. Behold what will be, in the end, without end! For what is our end, but to reach that kingdom which has no end.'

QUESTIONS FOR FURTHER REFLECTION

Prayer of St Augustine

O Lord my God,
my only hope,
hear me in your goodness:
grant that I may not stop seeking you when I am weary,
but seek your presence ever more fervently.
Give me the strength to seek you:
you allow yourself to be found
and inspire in me the hope of finding you
through an ever-increasing knowledge of you.
I lay before you my strength and my weakness:
preserve my strength and heal my weakness.
I lay before you
my learning and my ignorance;
where you open a door for me
welcome me as I go in,
and where one is closed
open it to me when I knock.

Let me always remember you,
understand you
and love you.
Increase your gifts in me
until in the end you transform me
into a new creation.

On the Trinity, XV, 28

For personal reflection

1. Read again the comments on our 'capacity for wonder' (see page 176). Do any particular experiences come to mind when you think about wonder? Perhaps there is a specific place or situation which regularly fills you with wonder. Close your eyes and take yourself there in your mind, and enjoy the experience by breathing it in deeply. Thank God for this expression of his love to you.

2. Henri Nouwen learned a great amount about faith and love from Adam, a severely handicapped young man (see page 177). Do you know someone who is handicapped in some way? Have you learned anything from them, or from the way their family relate to them? How do you react to handicapped people you meet on the street? Are you embarrassed, irritated, helpless, even a little bit unnerved? How do you think God sees them?

3. Look at your time line again. Are there any moments which you can see in retrospect have been for you the gentle breath of the Holy Spirit? These may be peak experiences, or it may have been guidance over a period of time.

4. How can we prepare for our own death? Would you want to plan your own funeral service? If you knew when you

were going to die, how would you spend the last six months of your life? Does your answer give you any thoughts about how you want to live, even though you believe you have a great deal longer to live than that?

For group discussion

1. Read 1 John 3:1–3, 19–24. These verses relate to the balance of worship and service (see Question D below) and loving the unlovable (see Question 2 above).
2. Work through the questions for personal reflection, sharing with the group anything that would be helpful.
3. Share your experience of worship in church. Is there any part of it which for you inspires wonder? Which parts demand a reaction from your head, and which from your heart? Does the worship in your church 'open doors ... onto a larger, transcendent world and an enriched life' (see page 183)? This is obviously an ideal: how can your church draw any closer to this?
4. Is our response to the presence of God 'one of loving service – in the high street as much as in the sanctuary' (see page 186)? Do you know people, or groups of people, who you feel have got out of balance in one way or the other? Where is your church on this spectrum? Where are you?
5. Share positive and negative experiences of death. Be aware that others may be hurting or coming to terms with a bereavement, and do not feel under pressure to share anything you are not ready to share.

Bible passage for meditation

This passage can increase our capacity for wonder, especially at the working of God in our life. If this is true all our life, may it not be so in death?

Psalm 139:7–12

Where can I go from your spirit?
Or where can I flee from your presence?
If I ascend to heaven, you are there;
if I make my bed in Sheol, you are there.
If I take the wings of the morning
and settle at the farthest limits of the sea,
even there your hand shall lead me,
and your right hand shall hold me fast.
If I say, 'Surely the darkness shall cover me,
and the light around me become night,'
even the darkness is not dark to you;
the night is as bright as the day,
for darkness is as light to you.

Epilogue

⌇

CHRISTIAN DISCIPLESHIP IN A MULTI-CULTURAL AND MULTI-FAITH SOCIETY

At this distance in time from the events of 11 September 2001, it is almost a truism to say that the rise of international terrorism that occasioned those events has changed the course of world history. It is typical of the record of history that from time to time events occur which, with the benefit of hindsight, we are able to see as decisive turning points in the human story. After such events, things are never quite the same again. Yet clearly the events in themselves are not the cause of the change, but rather the result of changes which have been going on for some time, largely unnoticed and certainly uncharted.

Without seeking to overexaggerate parallels in history, which is always a dangerous and dubious exercise, it might well be claimed that there are striking parallels (both symbolically and strategically) between the events of 11 September 2001 and the sack of Rome by Alaric the Goth in AD 410. On 24 August that year, the inconceivable happened: the Gothic army entered Rome and sacked it, burning extensive parts of the capital city of one of the greatest empires the world has known. 'It happened only recently,' wrote Pelagius, a monk from Britain, to a wealthy Roman lady. 'Rome, then mistress of the world, shivered, crushed with fear, at the sound of the blaring trumpets and the howling of the Goths ... Everyone was mingled together and shaken with fear; every household had its grief and an all-pervading terror gripped us.'[1] After all, Rome had been the symbol of a whole civilization, impregnable, towering like a great Colossus over the known world.

Surely the World Trade Center towers in New York and the Pentagon building in Washington DC are strong symbols of the most powerful nation in the world, a nation that has been largely protected – by both its geography and its size – from the ravages of war on its own turf, involving its own unarmed civilians. Not unlike the sack of Rome, the terrorist attack on America was inconceivable. 'If Rome can perish,' wrote Jerome after the events of August 410, 'what can be safe?' The same could be said of New York. Large parts of our world are now caught in the grip of fear for 'what is coming on the earth' (see Mark 13). Fear breeds fanaticism, which in its turn infuses fundamentalism with a new, dangerous and simplistic logic. It would seem that once again we stand at a crossroads in history, confronted by the options of faith or fear, a new enlightenment or a new dark age, a radical reappraisal of our cherished presuppositions or the refusal to move outside the confines of the culture we know.

As long ago as 1986, the Roman Catholic historian Adrian Hastings commented on the world situation at the close of the twentieth century and foresaw the oncoming crisis. He explicitly compared that imminent crisis with the world situation at the end of Augustine's life, when the Roman Empire was falling apart under the onslaught of the Barbarian invasions which would eventually herald the Dark Ages.

We are faced ... with an Augustinian predicament. When the Vandals are at the gates, then there are three possible responses. One is simply to despair of the Kingdom, of any ultimate meaning in the world or in human history; the second is to withdraw into a private sacral sphere, a closed community, monastic or charismatic, abandoning the struggle for the secular state as irredeemably corrupt; the third is to imitate Augustine himself, take a sombre view, but also a very long one, and retain in hope, but without much evidence a Christian concern for the redeemability of the totality of things. By the 1980s, a great many Christians were succumbing to the first choice, and a great many to the second, but rather a few were making ready for the long haul of the genuine Augustinian.[2]

When Rome was sacked, Augustine, by then a seasoned bishop of the Church with a worldwide reputation as a Christian leader and prophet, picked up the challenge of the momentous events. Far from retreating into a literary ivory tower, he strode out with pen in hand to write his political and theological manifesto. *De Civitate Dei* – 'The City of God' – was to fortify the Church for the ensuing Dark Ages and prepare it for the flowering of the Middle Ages and beyond. In practice, Augustine refused the first two options outlined by Adrian Hastings and instead took 'a sombre view, but also a very long one', retaining 'in hope ... a Christian concern for the redeemability of the totality of things'. Indeed, Augustine spelled this out when he wrote, 'I no longer desired a better world, because I was thinking of creation as a whole; and in the light of this more balanced discernment, I had come to see that higher things are better than the lower, but that the sum of all creation is better than the higher things alone.'[3] That is a 'long haul' if ever there was one!

Augustine also wrote a long letter to Paulinus of Nola in which he taunted the elegant Paulinus, who could apparently still afford to be 'otherworldly', living an 'Evangelic death', as he called it, shut away from the business of the world. Augustine said that this old tradition of withdrawal from the concerns of the world was no longer enough, as it had been in the first flush of his Christian conversion. He now knew that he was compelled to 'live among men, for their benefit'. 'It seems to me,' he wrote, 'that the uncertainty and difficulty that we encounter, springs from the one fact that in the midst of the great variety of men's habits and opinions ... we are having to conduct the affairs of a whole people – not of the Roman people on earth, but of the citizens of the Heavenly Jerusalem.' Christian discipleship must be lived out in a world of different and differing opinions, different faiths and conflicting cultural presuppositions.

RELOCATING CHRISTIAN WITNESS IN VARYING CULTURES

That is the challenge facing all Christian churches today, as we are compelled to move out of our past privileges and protections into a culture which no longer takes for granted the place of the Church in a multi-cultural, multi-faith society.

In the Western world, until comparatively recently, we cannot remember a time when Christianity was not at the centre of our culture and our civilization. Although historians would mark the end of 'Christendom' as occurring with the final break-up of the Holy Roman Empire and the breakdown of monolithic Catholic Christianity at the Reformation, the mystique of living in a Christian society and culture has lingered long. Yet suddenly – perhaps with the dawn of the new millennium, and perhaps even more in the aftermath of 11 September 2001 – it is very clear that Christianity no longer holds centre stage in a society of many faiths and no faith. In one sense, this is no new situation. After all, for the first three hundred years of its existence, the Christian Church was largely an illegal religion, unprotected by the state and even persecuted by the ruling authorities. Initially, perhaps, we may be tempted to copy the models of that persecuted Church, supposing quite wrongly that we come out of the Christian era by the same doors through which we first entered. Merely putting the clock back in a naive primitivism, however, will simply not work. C.S. Lewis made precisely this point in a lecture in 1954. He refuted the simplistic notion

> that the historical process allows mere reversal; that Europe can come out of Christianity 'by the same door as in she went' and find herself back where she was. It is not what happens. A post-Christian man is not a Pagan; you might as well think that a married woman recovers her virginity by divorce. The post-Christian is cut off from the Christian past and therefore doubly from the Pagan past.[4]

No, this is new territory, demanding radical reappraisals of what it means to live out the life of Christian discipleship in a post-Christian and postmodernist society. Mother Mary Clare put it this way:

> We must try to understand the meaning of the age in which we are called to bear witness. We must accept the fact that this is an age in which the cloth is being unwoven. It is therefore no good trying to patch. We must, rather, set up the loom on which coming generations may weave new cloth according to the pattern that God provides.

IDENTITY AND DIFFERENCE

Two things became quite clear in the aftermath of 11 September: first, that globalization is here to stay, and second, that isolationism in any form is no longer a realistic option. We are all in this together, whether we like it or not, and for better or worse. Bill Clinton summed this up in his outstanding Richard Dimbleby Lecture in 2001, significantly entitled 'The Struggle for the Soul of the Twenty-first Century'. He said that we could 'no longer delude ourselves that the harsh realities a world away are without real consequence for our own people ... All of us will have to develop a truly global consciousness about what our responsibilities to each other are and what our relationships are to be.'

In the course of that lecture, Clinton developed his theme with a particular emphasis on 'what our relationships are to be' with those who have different values and different faiths. 'Don't you think it's interesting,' he said, 'that in the most modern of ages, the biggest problem is the oldest problem of human society – the fear of the other. And how quickly fear leads to distrust, to hatred, to dehumanization, to death.' He went on, 'Think about how we all organize our lives in little boxes – man, woman, British, American, Muslim, Christian, Jew, Tory, Labour, New Labour, Old Labour ... Our little boxes are important to us. And indeed it is necessary; how could you navigate life if you didn't know the difference between a child and an adult, an African and an Indian, a scientist and a lawyer? We have to organize that, but somewhere along the way, we finally come to understand that our life is more than all these boxes we're in. And that if we can't reach beyond that, we'll never have a fuller life.'

Jesus came to show us something of what that fuller, richer life could mean in practice. Thus we see in the New Testament how Jesus refuses to live within any of the boxes currently in vogue, politically, religiously, socially or otherwise. Like the true radical that he was and is, Jesus is so secure at the centre of himself, so centred in God, that he can afford to go to the edges and cross over all the lines of difference without fear or compromise. We see it most vividly in his encounter with the Samaritan woman at the well. 'How is it,' exclaims the Samaritan woman, 'that you, a Jew, ask a drink of me, a woman of Samaria?' Note how John places in parenthesis the words, 'Jews do not share things in common with Samaritans,' as if to drive home the point more forcefully (John 4:9). Yet here is Jesus crossing all the lines of difference: gender, ethnic, religious, social and political. Furthermore, he manages to enter into a meaningful encounter with this woman. He starts by asking her to do something for him – he speaks from need and weakness, and in doing so opens up doors and windows which would normally have remained closed through fear and convention.

We are called as disciples of Jesus to live in a world and culture where there are many differences woven into the fabric of our global village, in which there are simply not enough islands of isolation to go round, and in which fences, however high and sturdy, cannot protect us from the proximity of noisy and incompatible neighbours. We do not need to be threatened by such differences, if we are securely centred in the One whom Augustine defines as 'an infinite circle whose centre is everywhere and whose circumference is nowhere'. When a person is centred in such a God, there can never exist anything approaching a ghetto mentality, or that exclusiveness which draws all its energies from what it stands against.

In a joint article in the London *Times* of 17 January 2002, the Archbishop of Canterbury, Dr George Carey, and the Principal of the Muslim College in London, Zaki Badawi, wrote about the importance of continuing dialogue and expressed the opinion that in our day 'one of the key challenges is how to handle difference. The "dignity of difference" is a challenging, but exciting reality we must all address in the conviction that our faith will not be diminished but enhanced.' They concluded, 'We can discover much that is good and true in those who are different from ourselves and at the same time can come to a deeper understanding of our own tradition.' In a multi-faith society, the journey of faith must 'involve building bridges of friendship and respect'. This aim and objective must be owned by all our faith communities at every level if we are ever to have a life worth living on this planet in the future. We shall do this best if we work in communities rather than in isolation.

COMMUNITIES OF FAITH

Alasdair Macintyre wrote,

> What matters at this stage is the construction of local forms of community within which civility and the intellectual and moral life can be sustained through the new dark ages which are already upon us. And if the tradition of the virtues was able to survive the horrors of the last dark ages, we are not entirely without grounds for hope. This time, however, the barbarians are not waiting beyond the frontiers; they have already been governing us for quite some time. And it is our lack of consciousness of this that constitutes part of our predicament. We are not waiting for a Godot, but for another – doubtless very different – St Benedict.[5]

To 'another St Benedict' we might want to add 'another St Hilda of Whitby': we are waiting for men *and* women of community. It is when we are living in community and in relationship that we are most human. After all, if we are created as human beings in the image and likeness of God, then when we are in community and in relationship we are reflecting most nearly the Godhead who has revealed himself as 'Persons in community'.

Augustine's spirituality was essentially built on and fostered by life in community. All his life, even during the years before his baptism, Augustine lived in some sort of community – what we might now call an 'extended family'. Of course, the culture of his day encouraged family life on a large scale in ways which the contemporary 'nuclear family' of the West would find almost overwhelming. What is quite clear, however, is that the self-serving and competitive individualism so rampant in our own culture would have appeared very strange to the people of North Africa in Augustine's day.

After Augustine was baptized, and in his subsequent years as priest and bishop, this natural affirmation of life in community deepened and became integral to all that he understood as the characteristic Christian lifestyle. So important was the concept and practice of community life to Augustine that around the year AD 397 he wrote his Rule – the famous Rule of St Augustine. By then he had already been through many years of experience in the corporate religious life, from the year of his return to Thagaste with his little group of friends from Italy. Later, as a priest, he founded a monastery for lay brothers in Hippo. Finally, as a bishop, he set up a monastery for clerics and lay brothers in his house in Hippo, and it was at that point that he wrote his Rule.

The basis for the Rule is the ideal of the Early Church in Jerusalem described in Acts 4:31–5. For Augustine, as for other community founders, to be the Church is to be in community. This lifestyle should not be regarded as a way of life for specialists, but rather as the normal expression of Christian discipleship. 'The reason for this was that [Augustine was] convinced that the orientation to one's own self and individualism formed the greatest obstacle to the realization of the gospel.' For Augustine, 'The first community of Jerusalem plays the role of an ancient dream which becomes an ideal for the present and for the future. We could characterize the Rule of Augustine as a call to the evangelical equality of all people. It voices the Christian demand to bring all men and women into full community.' It is only in community and in relationship that we realize both the fullness of our humanity and our likeness to the divine nature of the Godhead in whose image humanity is fashioned. Life in community offers an alternative lifestyle in eloquent opposition to the curses of our own age, just as it did in the age of Augustine. According to Augustine, the Christian community should offer 'an alternative by striving to build up a community that is not motivated by possessiveness, pride and power, but by love for one another.' It is not difficult to see how very relevant the Rule of Augustine is in our own day and in the culture of the West, torn by consumerism and greed, fuelled at every turn by strident individualism.

It is arguably the breakdown of communities that has been the greatest cause of the dehumanizing of our society in recent years. Real life is life in relationship, but isolation and alienation spell death. Individualism, the curse of postmodernism, is evident at all levels today. At discos, for example, no one can talk with anybody else because of the noise, and when people dance they do so in isolation or opposite another person of either gender, 'doing their own thing'. Technology, far from enhancing communication and community, will doubtless lead to greater and greater isolation. Bank clerks will be replaced by machines, shopping will be done through the Internet, and the personal touch will disappear everywhere as people retreat into a virtual reality increasingly remote from anything that might be described as real life.

In the midst of all this, fragile communities of faith – churches, parishes, call them what you will – could stand out and offer an alternative lifestyle: life in community and relationship, what Nadim Nassar calls 'the culture of God'. Enoch Powell once wrote, 'For the gospel is indeed a social gospel. The good news of the gospel is imparted to the individual only as a member of society. The most fundamental heresy of all is to imagine that the gospel is given to individuals or received by individuals or apprehended by individuals.'[6] Unfortunately, there is a strong tendency for some Christians to promote their faith in an individualistic and self-serving manner that is quite contrary to the teaching of the gospels and to anything we see in the description of the Early Church in the Book of Acts.

Little wonder, then, that Lesslie Newbigin claimed that 'the only hermeneutic of the gospel is a congregation of men and women who believe it and live by it'. It will surely be little communities of faith, living out the principles of gospel life, that will be able to communicate to a fragmented society the good news of the new life which Christian disciples should share, one with another. These communities of faith, however, must not degenerate into ghettos in isolation from the rest of society – a society which Christians are there to serve. They must be distinctive and different from the cultural presuppositions of the world around them, while remaining connected with the wider community in which they are placed, in the same way that yeast relates to dough.

The Prior of the Taizé community used to describe the distinctive witness of the Christian lifestyle as representing 'a sign of contradiction'. In a document from the early second century we have a description of what those early Christian communities looked like to the outside world of a largely alien and hostile society. Clearly the early Christians in their fragile communities were in every sense 'signs of contradiction'. The author of the *Letter to Diognetus* captures their paradoxical lifestyle very vividly:

Christians are not distinguishable from other people by
nationality or language or the way they dress. They do not
live in cities reserved to themselves; they do not speak a
special dialect; there is nothing eccentric about their way
of life. Their beliefs are not the invention of some sharp,
inquisitive mind, nor are they like some, slaves of this or
that school of thought. They are distributed among Greek
and non-Greek cities alike, according to their human lot.
They conform to local usage in their dress, diet, and manner of life.

Nevertheless in their communities they do reveal some
extraordinary and undeniably paradoxical attitudes. They live
each in his or her own native country, but they are pilgrims in
transit. They play their full part as citizens and are content to
submit to every burden as if they were resident aliens. For
them, every foreign country is home, and every homeland is
foreign territory.

They marry like everyone else. They beget children, but
they do not abandon them at birth. They will share their table
with you, but not their marriage bed. They are in the world,
but they refuse to conform to the ways of the world. They
pass their days on earth, but their citizenship is in heaven.
They obey the established laws, but in their way of life transcend all laws . . . In a word, what the soul is to the body,
Christians are to the world.

LIGHTS OF THE WORLD IN AGES OF DARKNESS

In his writings and in his lifestyle, as a bishop living in community, Augustine coached the Church of his day to be to the
world 'what the soul is to the body'. While it is quite clear
that much of his life's work was collapsing in ruins as he was
dying in AD 430, with the Vandals at the gates of Hippo,
Augustine had prepared the Church, perhaps unwittingly, to

live and to survive through the coming Dark Ages. He had prepared the Church to live without the privileges and protection of being the established religion of the mighty Roman Empire. With the onset of the Dark Ages, Christians would necessarily live as they had been commanded to live by their Master – as 'salt', 'light' and 'leaven', doing as Jesus had done at the outset, by their example pointing men and women to the kingdom of God. Augustine's great masterpiece, *De Civitate Dei*, was to serve as the new Highway Code for Christian communities of faith living in a hostile age.

Charles Colson writes of our own day in these prophetic and chilling words: 'We sense that things are winding down, that somehow freedom, justice and order are slipping away. Our great civilization may not yet lie in smouldering ruins, but the enemy is within the gates. The times seem to smell of sunset. Encroaching darkness casts long shadows across every institution in our land.' Many may well feel that such a depressing diagnosis and prognosis of the state of Western civilization is too pessimistic by far. Be that as it may, there can be no doubting the facts of the matter. Christianity, especially in the West, no longer enjoys the privileges or protection which it enjoyed in recent centuries. We are constantly and correctly reminded that Christians now live in a multi-cultural and multi-faith society, often facing either indifference or open hostility.

There is no way forward for the Christian Churches, however, in seeking merely to copy Augustine's prescriptions, or anybody else's for that matter. Whether we are entering a new dark age or not, the solution is not to copy slavishly what has gone before. Neither should we be too concerned about the self-preservation of institutional Christianity in the various forms we have known it throughout history. All that is needed to preserve and promote the essential ingredients in communities of faith is a band of men and women whose hearts God has touched and whose lives he is transforming; men and women regularly gathering together, if need be only in twos or threes, making Christ present through the working of the Holy Spirit through Word and sacrament, and strengthened by those graces, going, as G.K. Chesterton called it, 'gaily in the dark'.

Whether the future world proves to be kinder to the Church and life in general, or miserable and needy, or indifferent, or hostile, the challenge to Christians to be what Christ intended them to be – namely, lights in a darkened world – still holds good. Our part is not to judge or to assess at this point or at any other point in history. We must do as the very early cells of Christian life did in the hostile days of that first Jerusalem Church, and devote ourselves 'to the apostles' teaching and fellowship, to the breaking of bread and the prayers' (Acts 2:42). We must not retreat into ghettos cut off from the world and its pain, but must resolve to stand where Christ stands, in the midst of it all, in the mess of it all, in the mystery of it all. Be very wary of those who think they know 'the shape of the Church to come'. We do not need to know that, and we can afford a healthy agnosticism about Churchianity. Like Paul, our sole concern must be a resolve to 'know nothing . . . except Jesus Christ, and him crucified' (1 Corinthians 2:2).

In AD 430, as Augustine lay dying in his community house in Hippo, he must have been tempted to despair for the future life of the Church in a world that was falling apart at the seams. In many ways, observation through the lenses of common sense would certainly have indicated such a pessimistic prognosis. Yet with eyes of faith already raised to the New Jerusalem, the heavenly city, Augustine died peacefully, his last moments recorded by his biographer Possidius, present at the deathbed. At last, the restless heart had found its rest in God.

At the conclusion of his *Confessions*, Augustine offers this prayer:

> The voice of your Book, Lord, tells us about your resting on the Sabbath, so that we may read ahead of time how, after our own works are done, we too shall repose in you in the Sabbath of eternal life. For even then, you shall rest in us even as you now work in us. And thus shall our rest be yours, even as the works we do now are your works accomplished through us. But you, Lord, are always working and always at rest. You are good itself, you need no good other than yourself, and you are forever at rest, because you yourself are rest.

Amen.

Notes

Prologue

1. Michael Hewlett, 'Sing to him in whom creation found its shape and origin', *New English Hymnal,* no. 142, Canterbury Press, 1986.
2. Hippo, or Annaba, is situated in present-day Algeria.
3. Jonathan Sachs, *The Times,* 8 October 2001.
4. Rose Macaulay, *Towers of Trebizond,* Collins, 1956, p. 205f.
5. Peter Brown, *Augustine of Hippo,* Faber and Faber, 1967, pp. 173, 177.
6. Sermon 148.2.3.

An Introduction to Augustine

1. *Confessions,* 3.1.
2. Ibid.
3. Ibid.
4. *Confessions,* 4.2.
5. Ibid., 6.11.
6. Ibid., 6.4.
7. Peter Brown, *Augustine of Hippo,* Faber and Faber, 1967, p. 46.
8. C.R.C. Allberry, *A Manichaean Psalmbook,* Part II (Manichaean Manuscripts in the Chester Beatty Collection, vol. ii), 1938, p. 56.
9. *Viz de utilitate credudi (The Advantage of Believing),* Sherl treatise of Augustine, viii, 20.
10. Henry Chadwick, *Saint Augustine Confessions,* Oxford University Press, 1991, p. xxi.
11. *Confessions,* 10.27.
12. Sermon 344.4.

13. You could not possibly list the letters to Erasmas from Augustine – they are too many and not easily accessible. I have readily listed in the bibliography the main current books on Augustine which contain some of these.

Chapter One: Setting Out on the Journey

1. J.H. Newman, *An Essay on the Development of Christian Doctrine,* Penguin, 1974, p. 100.
2. C.S. Lewis, *A Grief Observed,* Faber and Faber, 1961, p. 53.
3. Peter Brown, *Augustine of Hippo,* Faber and Faber, 1967, p. 79f.
4. T.S. Eliot, *Selected Poems 1909–1962, Four Quartets,* 'East Coker', Part V, Faber and Faber, 1940.
5. C.S. Lewis, *The Four Loves,* Geoffrey Bles, 1960, p. 138f.
6. Eliot, *Four Quartets,* 'East Coker' III.
7. *Confessions,* 5.8.
8. Ibid.
9. Ibid., 5.15.
10. It is interesting to note that Christ was not portrayed to the popular imagination at that time as a suffering, crucified Saviour. Crucifixes, in fact, only came to be used as a central image of the faith in the Middle Ages. In the fourth century Christ was generally portrayed as the 'Great Word of God' and the 'Wisdom of God' – the image which most likely attracted Augustine.
11. Richard Rolle, *The Fire of Love,* Hodder and Stoughton Christian Classics, 1992, p. 52.
12. C.S. Lewis, *They Asked for a Paper,* 'The Weight of Glory', Geoffrey Bles, 1962, p. 197.
13. Ibid., p. 20.
14. *Confessions,* 10.27.

Chapter Two: Pursuing Our Heart's Desire

1. Augustine, *Studies in St John,* 26, 4.
2. Don Marquis, 'The lesson of the moth', quoted in *Prayer* (vol. 1) by Simon Tugwell, Veritas, 1974, p. 92.

3. Thomas Traherne, 'Desire' in *Selected Poems and Prose,* Penguin, 1991, p. 43.

4. Collect for the Fourth Sunday after Trinity in The Book of Common Prayer, 1662.

5. W.H. Carruth, *Each in His Own Tongue and Other Poems,* Putnam, 1908, p. 33.

6. Traherne, 'Desire', p. 43.

7. Quoted without reference in Peter Frauce, *Journey: A Spiritual Odyssey,* Chatto and Windus, 1998, p. 155.

8. Quoted in Raynor C. Johnson, *Nurslings of Immortality,* Hodder and Stoughten, 1957, p. 149.

9. Gregory of Nyssa, *The Life of Moses,* Book 2, Paulist Press, p. 239.

10. Hadewitch, *Poems in Couplets,* in *The Complete Works,* Paulist Press, 1978, pp. 10, 103–14.

11. William Shakespeare, *As You Like It,* 2.7.

12. Augustine, *Reflections on the Psalms: Psalm 31:5.*

13. Simone Weil, *Intimations of Christianity,* Routledge and Kegan, 1957, p. 46.

14. Douglas A. Rhymes, *Through Prayer to Reality,* The Upper Room, 1947, p. 46.

15. Mervyn Peake, 'Out of the Chaos of My Doubt', *Selected Poems,* Faber and Faber, 1972.

Chapter Three: Amazing Grace

1. *Confessions,* 8.7.17.

2. T.S. Eliot, *Four Quartets,* 'Burnt Norton', Part I, Faber and Faber, 1940.

3. *Trial by Jury,* 1875.

4. William Shakespeare, *Henry VII,* 3.2.

5. *Epistolae,* 143.2.

6. *Contra Academicos,* 1.2.6.

7. Ronald Rolheiser, *The Holy Longing: The Search for a Christian Spirituality,* Doubleday, 1999, p. 213.

8. *Confessions,* 9.5.

9. Shakespeare, *King Lear,* 5.3.
10. Sermon 169.13.
11. *Confessions,* 9.6.

Chapter Four: The Conversion of the Heart

1. Quoted by William Butler Yeats.
2. Sermon 154.5.3.
3. George Herbert, 'Let all the world in every corner sing', Hymn 394, *New English Hymnal,* Vol. 2, Norwich, Canterbury Press, 1986.
4. First Exhortation from the Communion Service in The Book of Common Prayer.
5. Collect for the Second Sundays in Lent in The Book of Common Prayer.
6. Sermon 175.1.
7. Letter 186.12.39.
8. Metropolitan Ignatios of Latakia, 'The Difference the Holy Spirit Makes', Ecumenical Council of Churches, Uppsala, 1968.
9. *Commentary on Psalm 88,* 11, 14.
10. *Commentary on Psalm 96,* 2.
11. Cyprian Smith, *The Path of Life,* Ampleforth Abbey, 1995, p. 140.
12. Matthew 11:28; John 3:16; 1 Timothy 1:15; 1 John 2:1.
13. *Theology and Joy,* SCM Press, 1973, p. 55.
14. *Confessions,* 1.9.14.
15. *Commentary on Psalm 141,* 4.
16. *Commentary on Psalm 52,* 8.
17. *Commentary on Psalm 49,* 5.
18. *Confessions,* 5.6.10.
19. Ibid., 10.27, 38.
20. *Sermons,* 114.1.
21. *Treatise on St John's Gospel,* 1, 264.
22. *Sermons,* 17.2.
23. Ibid., 19.2.

214

24. W. Temple, *Citizen and Churchman*, Eyre and Spottiswood, 1944, p. 101.
25. Gerard Manley Hopkins, 'God's Grandeur', 1877.

Chapter Five: Vocation and Sanctification

1. See, for example, Letter 11, 2.
2. Letter 10.1.
3. Peter Brown, *Augustine of Hippo*, Faber and Faber, 1967, p. 134.
4. Ibid., p. 135.
5. Epistle 18.
6. Brown, *Augustine of Hippo*, p. 137.
7. *Confessions*, 9.10.26.
8. Dorothy L. Sayers, *The Zeal of Thy House*, Victor Gollancz, 1938, p. 205f.
9. Donald Coggan, *Convictions*, Hodder and Stoughton, 1975, p. 272.
10. *Commentary on Psalm 40, 5*.

Chapter Six: The Point of It All

1. *On the Trinity*, 10.7.
2. Julian of Norwich, *Revelations of Divine Love*.
3. *Second Homily on First Letter of St John*.
4. Kenneth Leech, *The Sky is Red*, Darton, Longman and Todd, 1997, p. 114.
5. Dag Hammerskjöld, *Markings*, Faber and Faber, 1964, p. 64.
6. Henri J.M. Nouwen, *Finding My Way Home*, Darton, Longman and Todd, 2001, p. 67.
7. William Temple, *The Hope of a New World*, Macmillan, 1944, p. 31.
8. Colin Dunlop, *Anglican Public Worship*, SCM Press, 1953, p. 14.
9. Michael Marshall, *Free to Worship*, Marshall Pickering, 1996, p. 12.
10. Ibid., p. 6.

11. Temple, *The Hope of a New World*, p. 30.
12. William Temple, *Citizen and Churchman*, Eyre and Spottiswood, 1944, p. 101.
13. Possidius, *Life of Augustine*, XXVIII, 6–8.

Epilogue

1. Pelagius, *Letter to Demetriades*.
2. Adrian Hastings, *A History of English Christianity*, William Collins Sons, 1986, p. 660.
3. *Confessions*, 7.13.19.
4. C.S. Lewis, *De descriptione temporum* in *They Asked for a Paper*, Geoffrey Bles, 1962, p. 20.
5. Quoted in Kenneth Leech, *The Eye of the Storm*, Darton, Longman and Todd, 1992, p. 200.
6. Quoted in Kenneth Leech, *The Sky is Red*, Darton, Longman and Todd, 1997, p. 133.

Bibliography

St Augustine, *Confessions,* trans. Henry Chadwick, Oxford University Press, 1991.

Peter Brown, *Augustine of Hippo,* London, Faber and Faber, 1967.

Paula Clifford, trans., *Praying with Saint Augustine,* Triangle, 1987.

Serge Lancel, *St. Augustine,* London, SCM Press, 2002.

Michael Marshall, *The Restless Heart: The Life and Influence of St. Augustine,* Grand Rapids, Eerdmans, 1987.

Maura See, ed., *Daily Readings with St. Augustine,* Springfield, Ill., Templegate, 1986.

Paul Thigpen, comp., *Restless till We Rest in You: 60 Reflections from the Writings of St. Augustine,* Ann Arbor, Servant, 1998.

Frederic van der Meer, *Augustine the Bishop,* London, Sheed and Ward, 1961.

David Winter, ed., *The Wisdom of St. Augustine,* Oxford, Lion, 1997.

We want to hear from you. Please send your comments about this book to us in care of the address below. Thank you.

GRAND RAPIDS, MICHIGAN 49530 USA

WWW.ZONDERVAN.COM